THE
LITTLE
BOOK

OF

DALKEY AND
KILLINEY

HUGH ORAM

First published 2020

The History Press
97 St George's Place, Cheltenham,
Gloucestershire, GL50 3QB
www.thehistorypress.co.uk
© Hugh Oram, 2020

Photographs © Hugh Oram, 2020

British Library Cataloguing in Publication Data.
A catalogue record for this book is available from the British Library.

ISBN 978 0 7509 9216 9

Typesetting and origination by The History Press
Printed and bound in Great Britain by TJ International Ltd.

CONTENTS

ACKNOWLEDGEMENTS

I should especially like to thank my beloved wife, Bernadette, for all her help and encouragement during my writing career over the past four decades. I am indebted to various friends who have given me lots of encouragement and support while I was researching and writing this book: Thelma Byrne, Dublin; Christina Cannon, Dublin; Aisling Curley, Dublin; Miriam Doyle, Blackrock, Co. Dublin; Maria Gillen, Enniscrone, Co. Sligo, and Mary Murphy, Caherlistrane, near Tuam, Co. Galway. I am also grateful for the support of Michelle Clarke, her partner Kevin and their dog Freddie, in Ballsbridge, Dublin; the manager of Dalkey Castle heritage centre; Alissa Fitzsimons of the Australian embassy, Dublin; Tony O'Reilly, formerly of Providence Resources, as well as Fr John Sinnott of Our Lady of Good Counsel, Killiney. Many retail outlets and other organisations contributed to the book, especially the Gutter bookshop in Railway Road, Dalkey. Others that helped include the post offices in Dalkey and Killiney; the Bulloch Harbour protection association; the Church of the Assumption in Dalkey; the Dalkey Library and the National Library of Ireland; Dalkey News, Castle Street, Dalkey; Daisie Stone, Railway Road, Dalkey; Maxwell's Pharmacy, Castle Street, Dalkey; On the Grapevine, St Patrick's Road; Photogenic Photographers, Railway Road, Dalkey; Station House, Sorrento Drive, Dalkey; St Patrick's Dramatic Society, Dalkey, and the Sue Ryder Centre, Dalkey.

I also appreciate the warm memories, reminiscences and friendships I enjoyed with three Dalkey celebrities who sadly are no longer with us – Maeve Binchy, Hugh Leonard and Theodora FitzGibbon. The technical assistance of Dean Lochner of the Bondi Group, Ballsbridge, Dublin, has been invaluable.

INTRODUCTION

Dalkey has been around a long time, some 1,500 years to be precise, as evidenced by St Begnet's churchyard in Castle Street. On the other hand, Killiney is a much more recent upstart, since it only started to develop after the railway had arrived in 1858. But in recent years, both Dalkey and Killiney have consolidated their positions as the most expensive places in Ireland to buy a house. To buy a decent sized house, either old or new, in either place, you'll need at least a cool €5 million in your wallet or purse.

However, Dalkey's medieval history is impressive. From about 1300 onwards, the River Liffey was so silted up that it couldn't be used as a port for Dublin, so Dalkey stood in. Goods were either unloaded in Dalkey and taken by packhorse to Dublin (the forerunner of the DART) or transshipped to Ringsend, which in those days was a small coastal village some distance from Dublin.

Residents' strong attachment to the sea is seen today in the ferocious attachment they have to Bulloch Harbour and the energy they put into preventing unwanted developments. The much smaller Coliemore Harbour, from which boats depart to the delightfully natural and unspoiled Dalkey Island, also has a strong resonance with the Dalkey community.

Dalkey developed strong fortifications, including seven castles, two of which survive today, in Castle Street. During the nineteenth century, Dalkey began to develop as a proper village and today, a couple of retail establishments in Dalkey date back to the late nineteenth century. Dalkey has also seen the development of many communal facilities, such as the library and St Mary's Hall, both on Castle Street. Such is the attachment of people in the area to the unspoiled village charms of Dalkey's central area that multinationals who've tried to plant footholds in the area, such as Starbucks, have met with a frosty reception. After the railway arrived in Dalkey, house building accelerated and many fine residential developments took place during the nineteenth century, such as the magnificent Sorrento Terrace. On the other hand, Killiney has had to work harder to create a separate identity. Until the Vico Road was opened up in the mid-nineteenth century, Killiney had no north–south road apart from Killiney Hill Road. It still lacks a pivotal village centre to match that of Dalkey, and it doesn't have the retail and communal facilities of Dalkey. Places like Killiney Shopping Centre, while useful, don't have the same zeitgeist as Dalkey's Castle Street. However, both areas have had a strong attraction for artists of all kinds, whether writers, painters or musicians. In Killiney, beyond doubt, the best-known artistic resident is Bono of U2, while another band member, 'The Edge', also lives in the area. In Dalkey, by contrast, the village has been popular with many writers, such as George Bernard Shaw and in much more modern times, Maeve Binchy and Hugh Leonard, while well-known contemporary media performers, such as Vincent Browne, have long been attracted to Dalkey's delights.

The unspoiled natural attractions have a powerful appeal. Dalkey Island is a wonderful place to escape the fast pace of modern life, while for rock climbers, Dalkey's old quarry is one of the best and most challenging spots in the country. Killiney Hill also provides stiff challenges for walkers and those who like slightly more modest uphill ventures.

In terms of public transport access, since the DART arrived in 1984, both Dalkey and Killiney have been easy to reach. Dalkey has long since overcome the withdrawal of its Number 8 tram service to Dublin city centre, in 1949, and the much more recent withdrawal of the Number 8 bus in 2015.

TIMELINE

c. 650   First church on Dalkey Island
1200   Dalkey becomes the main harbour for Dublin and remains so for four centuries
1326   Archbishop of Dublin grants thirty-nine burgages in Dalkey
1740   Killiney Obelisk built
1745   The Queens Bar and Hotel, Castle Street, Dalkey, opens
1757   Dalkey is described as having seven castles
1780   First King of Dalkey is crowned
1798   About 1,000 insurgents gather on Dalkey Hill for the rebellion
1815   Start of quarrying at Dalkey Hill, for building of Kingstown Harbour
1818   Construction starts on Bulloch Harbour
1840   Manderley Castle, now owned by the Irish singer-songwriter Enya, is built
1840   Church of the Assumption, Dalkey, is built
1843   St Patrick's Church of Ireland, Dalkey, is built
1843   Loreto Abbey, Dalkey, is founded
1844   Atmospheric railway is built in Dalkey
1845   Construction begins on Sorrento Terrace
1847   Queenstown Tavern opens at Coliemore Road, Dalkey (now The Club)
1854   Dalkey railway station opens
1858   First station opens at Killiney (present station opens in 1882)
1858   Holy Trinity church, Killiney, is built

1866   George Bernard Shaw moves into Torca Cottage, Dalkey; he lives there for eight years

1869   The Goat Castle, Dalkey, is turned into the town hall

1887   Killiney Hill Park, formerly Victoria Park, opens

1889   Vico Road opens as a public thoroughfare

1904   James Joyce teaches for a term at Clifton School, Dalkey Avenue

1949   Last tram route, the number 8 to Dalkey, closes down

1958   Lennox Robinson, playwright, producer and long-time resident at Sorrento Cottage in Dalkey, dies

1964   *The Dalkey Archive*, a comic novel by Flann O'Brien, is published

1966   After Nelson's Pillar in O'Connell Street, Dublin is blown up, Nelson's head is used in a fashion photoshoot on Killiney beach

1970   Dan Finnegan buys what is now Finnegan's pub, Dalkey

1973   Dalkey Community Council is founded

1975   Rolland's Restaurant opens in Killiney

1979   Two trains collide near Dalkey; over forty people are injured

1984   DART rail system opens and includes Dalkey and Killiney stations

1991   Theodora FitzGibbon, food writer and critic, who lived for many years at Coliemore Road, Dalkey, dies

1993   Cyril Cusack, actor, who had close connections with Dalkey, dies

1998   Heritage Centre opens in Dalkey Castle

1998   Jim Sheridan, film-maker, buys site for seafront home in Dalkey

2002   Paddy Fitzpatrick, owner of Fitzpatrick's Castle Hotel, Killiney, dies

2003   Harry Latham, chronicler of Dalkey history, dies

2006   Killiney Court Hotel closes down

2006   Dr John de Courcy Ireland, marine historian who lived at Dalkey Avenue for many years, dies

2009   Hugh Leonard, playwright and novelist, raised in Dalkey and long-time resident at Pilot View, Dalkey, dies

2012   Maeve Binchy, author and long-time Dalkey resident, dies

2015   End of Dublin Bus Number 8 route to Dalkey

2017   The Guinea Pig restaurant, Dalkey, is sold by Mervyn Stewart after forty years

2018   Killiney Stores, at the corner of Strathmore Road and Killiney Hill Road, closes

2018   Val Mulkerns, Dalkey-based writer, dies

2019   The Second World War sign at Hawk Cliff, Dalkey, is restored

1

CHURCHES

CHURCH OF THE ASSUMPTION, DALKEY

This church, on Castle Street in Dalkey, was built in 1840 and 1841. The first parish priest of the parish of Kingstown, formed in 1829 and running from Kingstown to Bray, was Canon Sheridan. In March 1840, he called a meeting of Dalkey residents to discuss building a new church in Dalkey. As a result of that meeting, a site was leased from Thomas Connolly, opposite the ruins of St Begnet's. Later on, Connolly's son, Canon James Connolly, who was the parish priest of St Kevin's in Harrington Street, Dublin, donated the site in Castle Street to the new church. The church was built from granite, in the Gothic Revival style, and when it was dedicated on 26 September 1841, it consisted only of the present-day nave. It wasn't until Dalkey was expanding, in the 1880s, that the then parish priest decided to extend the church, adding new transepts, as well as a bell tower. The roof was raised, a fan vaulted ceiling was added, and an organ was installed.

Over the next fifty years, many more interior decorations were added. Then, in 1991, the church was renovated for its 150th anniversary. The French-made stained-glass windows were restored and the plaster Stations of the Cross were returned to their original colour. Today, the two priests at the church are Fr Patrick Devitt, the administrator, who celebrated his golden jubilee as a priest in June 2019, and Fr Declan Gallagher. Finbarr Madden is the sacristan and Caitriona Fogarty is the parish secretary. The parish's

Pastoral Council was set up in 2006 as a partnership between priests and laity. Among the many funerals held at the church in recent years was that of author Maeve Binchy in 2012, when it was said that she was up talking with the Almighty.

DALKEY PARISH OUTREACH

This was set up in 1999 by Terry Dunne and Clare Byrne, who discovered that even small amounts of money can do an amazing amount of good. Out of that project evolved the Friends of Kitui, a voluntary group that encouraged development projects in the Catholic diocese of Kitui in Kenya. The group lasted until 2012.

HOLY TRINITY CHURCH, KILLINEY

This Church of Ireland church, built in 1859, is set in a corner of Killiney Hill Road. It was built three years after the railway line was built through Killiney and its arrival encouraged the building of many new houses, hence the new church. The church was built on part of the grounds of Killiney Castle and its then owner, Robert Warren, put up most of the money for the construction of the church. His nephew, Sandham Symes, was the architect.

Tucked in under the slope of Killiney Hill, the church has a short tower, topped with a curious Oriental-looking copper cap. The church is renowned for its Harry Clarke stained-glass window, the Angel of Peace; visitors come from all over the world to see it. The church also has a magnificent carved pulpit with five bronze panels. The current rector is the Venerable Gary Hastings.

Across the road from the church is the Carry Centre, which is a hub of community and parochial activities throughout the week.

LORETO ABBEY, DALKEY

Loreto Abbey is a member house of the Institute of the Blessed Virgin Mary, which was founded in the seventeenth century.

Loreto College, Dalkey.

Loreto Abbey, Dalkey.

The Irish branch of the Institute was founded in 1821 by Frances Ball. She founded Loreto Abbey in 1841 and designed the castellated structure, built from Dalkey granite, herself. The abbey opened as a day and boarding school in 1843.

OUR LADY OF GOOD COUNSEL, BALLYBRACK

One of the newer churches in the area, the parish was constituted from Cabinteely parish in 1974 and the new church was built at Church View Road, Killiney, shortly afterwards. The pastoral centre was built in 2007 and remains a vibrant hub for the parish, where the current priest is Fr John Sinnott. St Stephen's is a chapel of ease to the Ballybrack church. It was opened in 1984 and Imogen Stuart became the artist in residence. The interior of the chapel of ease is tranquil and simple, while outside, the small garden with its mini cloisters also conveys an impression of monastic serenity. However, recent staffing difficulties in the Roman Catholic Church have meant that the opening times for the chapel of ease can be sporadic.

ST BEGNET'S CHURCH RUINS

Directly opposite the Church of the Assumption in Dalkey are the ruins of St Begnet's Church. St Begnet, or St Becnat, is the patron saint of Dalkey, but little is known of her. In the eleventh century, she was said to have been a member of the aristocratic family of Dál Messin Corb, which ruled over north and central Leinster until about 700 AD. When they lost control over these territories, their rule was confined to the Wicklow Mountains. As for St Begnet, she established churches both in Dalkey itself and on nearby Dalkey Island. The ruins of both can be seen today; in the case of the Dalkey ruins, those are next door to Dalkey

St Begnet's graveyard, Castle Street, Dalkey.

Castle and its heritage centre. The area around the Dalkey church was used as a burial ground from the thirteenth century onwards and the last burial took place in 1930. The earliest part of the church ruins date from the tenth century. Before the stone church was built, there was probably a wooden church on the site during the sixth or seventh centuries.

ST MATTHIAS, BALLYBRACK

This Church of Ireland church at Church Road, Ballybrack, dates back to the 1840s. The exterior of the church is noted for its deep-set and narrow doors and windows, as well as its pinnacles. The church is cruciform in its design, including a nave with transepts and a chancel with the bell tower at the west end. The windows are of late Victorian stained glass. There's also a large parish centre, with three rooms and parking for fifty cars. The rector is Revd Dr William Olhausen, while the honorary curate is Revd Paddy McGlinchey.

ST PATRICK'S CHURCH, DALKEY

This Church of Ireland church dates back to 1843, shortly after the Roman Catholic church in Castle Street, Dalkey, was consecrated. St Patrick's was built on a granite outcrop overlooking Bulloch Harbour and it has remained a landmark in the area ever since. The current rector is Revd Bruce Hayes. The sermon at the opening service in 1843 was preached by Richard Whately, the highly eccentric Church of Ireland Archbishop of Dublin. The church was extended in 1853 and again in 1879. The adjoining schoolhouse had been built in 1870. In 1999, the whole parochial hall complex was upgraded and extended and a new school building added.

Today, the interior memorials remain one of the most interesting points of the church's interior. They include a memorial to local people who fell during the First World War of 1914 to 1918. The adjoining rectory was built in 1866 in the Russian villa style which was then so popular.

St Patrick's Church, Dalkey.

It was built on the site of a disused quarry, which had provided the stone for the church itself. One of the features of the rectory garden was the vast number of rosebushes, 400 in all, long since gone, but which continue to flourish in the gardens of parishioners.

2

COMMUNITY ORGANISATIONS

DALKEY ACTIVE RETIREMENT ASSOCIATION

The association, which is part of the Dalkey parish of the Assumption of the Blessed Virgin Mary, has over 500 members. It is open to people aged over 55 who live in Dalkey and it provides a wide range of cultural, educational, social and sporting activities, and encourages people to have positive attitudes towards ageing and retirement. The association has an office in Our Lady's Hall and a full list of activities is displayed on the noticeboard in the window of the hall. New members are inducted every September.

DALKEY LITERARY, HISTORICAL AND DEBATING SOCIETY

One of the old-time community organisations in Dalkey, it caused considerable controversy at one of its meetings, held at the end of August 1960. A former Nazi commando, Colonel Otto Skorzeny, was invited to speak, despite many calls to withdraw the invitation. US General Eisenhower, who later became a US President, once said that Skorzeny was the most dangerous man in Europe. After the defeat of Nazi Germany in 1945, Skorzeny spent three years in prison before escaping.

Dalkey library, Castle Street, Dalkey.

DALKEY LIBRARY

The Dalkey branch library at Castle Street was recently refurbished. It has an excellent stock of books, including in its junior library, while events there include meetings of its book club. The garden is dedicated to Maeve Binchy.

DALKEY'S MASONIC LODGE

Dalkey has long had a Masonic presence, as indicated by the plaque on the wall of Number 9, Castle Street, which shows that a Masonic Lodge was established there in 1873. During the 1922/3 civil war, the Greystones Orange Hall, home of the Masonic Lodge, was burned down. Until it was rebuilt in 1925, the lodge met at the Dalkey lodge 261. Much more recently, one of the Bray lodges moved to the Masonic Hall in Dalkey. Today, the Masonic Lodge in Dalkey is still active.

DALKEY TIDY TOWNS COMMITTEE

The Dalkey Tidy Towns committee works hard to ensure that the town stays clean and litter free, to maintain its excellent record in the annual Tidy Towns competition. In April 2019, the committee caused controversy when it said it would remove and destroy any election posters put up in the town. Election candidates were advised not to put up single-use plastic election posters.

KILLINEY DISTRICT COMMUNITY COUNCIL

The council represents and promotes the interests of residents, businesses, clubs and organisations in the Killiney area.

OUR LADY'S HALL, DALKEY

This community facility in Castle Street is widely used by the local community. It is used, for instance, by the Active Retirement Association for over 50s, as well as Dalkey Community Council's annual art exhibition. The Community Council's newsletter was first published in 1974, making it the longest running voluntary community newsletter in Ireland.

Other events in the hall include Dalkey parish's outreach coffee mornings, held on the last Sunday of every month.

ST PATRICK'S DRAMATIC SOCIETY, DALKEY

The society was founded in 1961, making it one of the longest running of its kind in Ireland. Its season runs from September to May, during which time the society puts on a three-act autumn production, as well as two plays each of one act and a three-act play in the spring. The society also takes part in the One Act circuit, the Bray One Act Festival and other events.

Its productions are staged in the Northover Hall, Dalkey; Dalkey town hall and venues in Dún Laoghaire.

For the 2018/19 season, the society was chaired by Seymour Cresswell, while the five-strong committee was made up of Deirdre Burke, Odette Colgan, Fiona Darling, Michael Fogarty and Hannah Blair White. The treasurer was William Mansfield and the secretary was Hilda Grace.

DALKEY COMMUNITY COUNCIL

The Dalkey Community Council, which came into being in 1974, reflects the great variety of community organisations in the area and has the following guiding principles: to increase community harmony and fellowship of all the people living in Dalkey, regardless of their social stature, and to facilitate and foster facilities in the interests of social wellbeing, health, recreation and leisure.

The origins of the Council go back to 1973, when the Dalkey Ladies' Club was set up to bind together the various organisations representing women in the town. At the time, the area had many young families and the mothers in particular were keen to integrate into the life of the area. The development of the Ladies' Club also inspired interest in the creation of a community-wide organisation. Questionnaires were sent out to every house in Dalkey and comments requested. Following that, an election was held to elect representatives to a proposed council that would represent all the organisations in Dalkey as well as its geographical areas. The details of what was happening in Dalkey were published in *The Irish Times* and this led to a letter from the then President, Erskine Childers, offering to help the newly formed council in any way he could.

In 1974, the Dalkey Community Council was formally launched at a ceremony in the sports centre at Hyde Road;

President Hillery did the honours in launching the new council. Over 500 people attended the meeting. The first chairperson was Peter Northover, while the vice-chairs were Mrs Doris Smyth and Martin Kennedy. The secretary was Mrs Mai Kelly, while the assistant secretary was Mrs Eithne Dooge. The treasurer was Robin Budd, while Harry Latham was appointed pro and Richard Blake the assistant pro.

The same week that the Community Council was launched, a house fire at Carysfort Road in Dalkey claimed the lives of all but two members of the Howard family. This dreadful event galvanised local support from all parts of the community and from all local organisations to get behind the new Dalkey Community Council.

Another early decision of the Council was to publish a local newsletter. The first issue came out in April 1974 and it has continued ever since, making it the longest published community newsletter in Ireland. The Dalkey Community Council maintains an online database of previous issues so that people can have easy access to a vast array of content. The newsletter continues to be well supported by local businesses.

Since it was set up nearly fifty years ago, the Dalkey Community Council has continued to expand the wide variety of interests it promotes, enhancing life for all the residents of Dalkey.

DALKEY AND THE TIDY TOWNS COMPETITION

Dalkey has long taken part in the Tidy Towns competition and its marks have soared ever upwards since the lowest point, in 1999. The remarks made by the adjudicators in the 2013 competition give a good indication of how much progress Dalkey has made in the competition over the years. The town first entered the competition in 1983 and it was pointed out that the Dalkey committee for the competition is a very representative group for all parts of the community and works for the betterment of the town as a whole. The various business entities in Dalkey are closely involved and so too are over a dozen community groups, including the famed Cuala GAA club in Dalkey.

One of the adjudicators noted in 2013 that it had been quite a while since he had visited Dalkey and its idyllic surroundings, taking in both Bulloch Harbour and Coliemore Harbour. He noted the great diversity in the built environment, with many larger properties, some of significant historical interest. On the cliff end of the village, the attractive cottage terrace type homes on St Patrick's Road were of equal historical interest, as they represented a time when Dalkey was very much a dependent fishing village. The adjudicating team were also very impressed by the heritage centre in Dalkey Castle, representative of Dalkey's unique attractions as a heritage town in the greater Dublin area.

The very striking St Patrick's Anglican church and grounds were described as being quite impressive, while the famed Loreto Abbey and grounds looking out towards the Martello tower on Dalkey Island were in a good state of preservation, while at that stage, in 2013, the nearby national school was getting an extension. Coliemore Harbour looked secluded and resplendent, with some fine stonework and cobblestones. But the 2013 adjudicators noted that the once vibrant building that was Queenstown Castle looked run down. It had a 'for sale' sign up and it was assumed that it would take quite a packet to restore it to its former glory.

Among the new additions noted in Dalkey in 2013 were the new tourist map outside the Church of the Assumption on Castle Street, new stone planters, improvements to areas at the DART station and the Dalkey Wayfinder project, with some new bilingual signs. The Harry Latham memorial seat was admired for the simplicity of its design. A number of commercial premises appealed to the adjudicator for reasons of simple design, both traditional and contemporary, including Eurospar, Our Lady's Hall, Kerins pharmacy, McDonaghs, which is synonymous with Dalkey, Ouzos, No. 2 opticians, and a number of private houses.

The layout of Dalkey lends itself to good landscaping. The addition of more trees in the grounds of the Loreto Abbey school was noted, while the themed Maeve Binchy Peace Garden was described as a well-deserved recognition for someone who had done so much to put Dalkey on the map. However, the green area at Dillon Park was quite bare and wasn't being exploited fully. However, some lovely wildflower arrangements were seen in Sorrento Park and at the Cat's Ladder. New and attractive information boards at locations like Coliemore Harbour were recommended.

The adjudicators pointed out that Dalkey is a town of contrasts when it comes to residential properties. There are plenty of larger, gated residences, while in the heart of the town, there are the very attractive cottages on St Patrick's Road. The adjudicator traversed such areas as St Begnet's Villas, Church Road, Hyde Road, Ballinaclea Road and Ardeevin Road, going on to Sorrento Terrace and the Coliemore and Vico roads. One thing that all the houses had in common is that they are maintained to a very high standard, some with exquisite gardens, a credit to their owners. Name signs were clear and visible and the footpaths were accessible.

It was also pointed out that the approaches to the town are in a very presentable condition, helped in no small way by the absence of interjunctions and roundabouts. The main street and the road network within the town are easy enough to get around, although the roads in the hilly areas are narrow and caution is always needed when driving around them.

The waste management policies were commended, especially the strategy for paperless communications. The standard of tidiness throughout Dalkey was also commended, although there were exceptions, like Bulloch Harbour and Sorrento Park. But overall, generally high standards have been achieved in what the adjudicators described as an impressive heritage town.

3

CRIME AND MAYHEM

NELSON'S HEAD

Nelson's Pillar near the GPO in O'Connell Street, Dublin, was blown up in an explosion carried out by a republican sympathiser, in March 1966. The only piece of the statue that remained intact was Nelson's head, which the old Dublin Corporation put into storage at its Clanbrassil Street depot. Students of the National College of Art & Design stole it from the depot and for six months, Nelson's head had a wandering existence, appearing at various venues in Dublin and even in an antiques shop in London.

One of its most bizarre appearances was on Killiney beach during the summer of 1966, when it appeared as a prop for a fashion photoshoot on the beach. Subsequently, the head was recovered and was stored for many years by Dublin Corporation at a depot in Ardee Street. Finally, in 2005, it was put on display at Pearse Street Library, where it can still be seen today.

POST OFFICE RAID IN DALKEY

In October 1922, there were two raids on the railway station at Dalkey, by republicans who seized mail bags. On the first occasion, about 300 letters were taken but were returned two hours later. All the letters had been opened and were marked 'Censored by the IRA'. In the second raid, the stolen letters were subsequently recovered on the Knocknacree Road in Dalkey.

WAR OF INDEPENDENCE, 1919–1921 AND IRISH CIVIL WAR, 1922–23

The War of Independence and the Civil War had but a slight impact on the wealthy citizens of Dalkey and Killiney, as well as their poorer compatriots, especially in the Dalkey area.

A local man, Paddy D'Arcy, was made commanding officer of the Old IRA, in charge of a dozen recruits. Especially during the Civil War, they tried to make an impact, but largely failed. They attacked the Free State military post on Killiney Hill over twenty times, without causing much damage. During one of their earliest ambushes, on 19 May 1920, the gang murdered William J. McCabe, the head gardener at Marino, one of the big houses in Killiney. The ambush took place at the foot of Victoria Hill, Killiney.

In October 1922, they smashed up the telephone exchange in Killiney and also robbed the accountant for the local urban district council of £350 in cash.

The demise of the Dalkey Flying Column came in March 1923, when it was cornered in a house at Albert Road, Glenageary. An Old IRA man was killed and so too was a soldier in the new national army. As for Paddy D'Arcy, he stayed on the run until July 1924, when he finally returned home. He stayed in the shadows for the rest of the 1920s, but after Fianna Fáil first came to power in 1932, he was reinstated to his old job in the civil service. He lived out the rest of his life demurely in Dalkey.

DIRECT PROVISION CENTRE

In April 2019, a poll was carried out in Dalkey by a local group that thought the area should get a direct provision centre. They said that since Dalkey is 98 per cent white, and largely old Irish stock, the town would be an ideal place for such a centre. A total of 382 people took part in the poll and 73 per cent agreed with the suggestion that the wealthy Dalkey areas should be considered for a Direct Provision Centre, instead of the usual less well-off areas that normally get such facilities.

Some of the comments that were included with the poll result were amusing. One respondent said that the centre should be built on a brownfield site opposite Pat Kenny's house, while another suggested that since Dalkey isn't far from Bono's home in Killiney, they could all go to the pub together.

BOMBING AND AMBUSHES

During the period of civil war in Ireland, ambushes and other events in the area were widely reported in *The Irish Times* and other Dublin newspapers of the era. The following are just three such articles from around Dalkey:

Scene of fatal motor smash near Dalkey, 23 Novmber 1922

A shocking motor accident occurred near Dalkey, Co. Dublin, at an early hour yesterday morning, when Lieutenant McKenna of the national army, was driving with a party of soldiers from the Harbour Barracks, Kingstown, along the Ulverton Road, towards Dalkey.

When about 40 yards from the scene of the recent fatal ambush [see below], and near the entrance to Bulloch Castle, the steering gear apparently went out of order and the Crossley tender collided with a tramway standard on the left-hand side of the road. The standard was smashed and the tender was completely wrecked, with the wheels and axles being broken and the bodywork reduced to matchwood.

Sergeant Thomas Doyle, a native of Newtownmountkennedy, Co. Wicklow, was killed instantly, his skull fractured by striking the roadway. Volunteer Thomas Whelan received severe injuries to the head and hip. The other occupants of the tender fortunately escaped with slight injuries.

The dead soldier and Volunteer Whelan were removed to the residence of Dr McClintock, at Dreghorn, Ulverton Road, where they were seen by Revd Father Fitzpatrick from Dalkey parish. Subsequently, the injured Volunteer was conveyed by military ambulance to Monkstown hospital, where he was received by Dr Weldon, the house surgeon, and detained as a patient. The body of Sergeant Doyle was removed to St Michael's Hospital, Kingstown.

Dalkey Ambush: a Verdict of Murder, 15 November 1922

Yesterday, at St Michael's Hospital, Kingstown, Dr J.P. Brennan, coroner for south Co. Dublin, held an inquest on the bodies of Mr H.A. Manning of Pilot Cottages, Dalkey, and Corporal Samuel Webb of the national army, a native of Kingstown, who were killed in an ambush at Ulverton Hill, Dalkey, on Monday night last. Mr M.A. Corrigan, chief State solicitor, appeared for the authorities, and Superintendent Kelleher for the Metropolitan Police.

The coroner, in opening the proceedings, said that the circumstances reported to him were that at 10.55 p.m. on the 15th inst., Privates Kavanagh and McNally with five other soldiers, were proceeding along Ulverton Road with a prisoner named John Keys when they were attacked with bombs, rifle and revolver fire from a field at Ulverton Road. Corporal George Webb and a civilian, whose supposed name was H.J. Manning, were taken to St Michael's hospital in Kingstown and pronounced dead by Dr Hesham, the house surgeon. Privates Sharkey and Leo Treston, who were with the patrol, were also injured and are now patients at Monkstown Hospital. Evidence of identification in the case of Mr Manning was given by Mr William Francis Waterhouse, Claremount, Killiney, who said that the deceased man was his brother-in-law, aged 43 and unmarried. He had spent Monday evening with the witness and left the house between 10.30 and 10.40 to go to his lodgings at Pilot Cottages, Bullock Harbour.

Margaret Kelly, 19, Library Road, Kingstown, identified the body of Corporal Webb as that of her brother-in-law, who was aged about 20 years and who was unmarried. Captain Keane of the Harbour Barracks in Kinsgtown stated that he had received a telephone message, as a result of which he went to Ulverton Road, the scene of the attack. A civilian stopped the car and the witness got out about 50 yards from the scene. Private Sharkey was lying on the road and a civilian was lying against the wall on the side of the road. An ambulance then came on the scene and removed the wounded. The witness found an unexploded bomb lying on the road.

Private Art O'Connor, from the Harbour Barracks, said that he was one of a patrol from the Barracks in Dalkey at about 11 p.m. When they reached the portion of the road where the rocks were protruding, rifle fire was opened on the patrol from the direction of the rocks. The witness lay down on the tram tracks. There was a bomb thrown, which exploded at the corner nearest to Kingstown. He saw Private Sharkey fall at the right side of the road. There was a civilian near him, who was also killed. A good deal of firing took place and another bomb was thrown, which exploded. The men were killed by the fire from the rocks.

Dr Michael J. Harty of St Michael's Hospital, said that he received the body of Private Samuel Webb. On examination, he found wounds on the left hand, a wound on the inner side of the left foot, near the ankle, and a penetrating wound on the right side. There was also a penetrating wound to the lower part of the right lobe of the right lung and the liver was also penetrated. Death was due to shock from the wounds.

In the coroner's opinion, the principal wound was caused by a bullet and not by a bomb splinter. The witness added that he had also received the body of Mr Manning and had found a punctured wound to the left ear, entering the skull and traversing the brain. Death was due to laceration of the brain caused by a .45 revolver bullet.

Lieutenant Commandant Joseph Flanagan of the Harbour Barracks, having described the finding of the bodies and their removal, said that when he arrived, the police handed him a bomb (produced in evidence) which had been picked up and put in a bucket of water. They later got two other bombs that had not exploded and seventeen empty and eight live rifle cartridges. Police Constable Joseph Keating, who searched the ambush scene, found an unexploded bomb behind the rocks where the ambushers had been, as well as seventeen empty cartridge cases and eighteen live cartridges. Mr Corrigan, the chief State solicitor, said that it was clear from witness accounts that these two men, a civilian and a national soldier, had been killed in the attack and that the people responsible were guilty of murder.

The coroner, in reviewing the evidence, said that this was another of the very regrettable tragedies they had to inquire into where one Irishman was up in arms against another brother Irishman and that there was no decent Irishman who did not regret it. With the morality of the acts of the belligerents the jury had no concern there and they had to arrive at their verdict upon the evidence before them. Mr C. Murphy, managing director of Messrs Clery & Co., for whom Mr Manning worked, expressed regret on behalf of himself and the firm at the death of Mr Manning. In his case, the jury found that death had been caused by a bullet fired by some person or persons unknown, and tendered sympathy to his relatives. In the case of Corporal Webb, a verdict that the deceased soldier was wilfully murdered by some person or persons unknown was returned. They tendered deep sympathy to the relatives of the deceased, in which the coroner and Mr Corrigan joined.

Bomb Thrown in Dalkey, 9 December 1922

Shortly after midnight, a bomb was thrown at a tender containing national troops passing along Ulverton Road in Dalkey, from the rocks at the side of the road. The missile exploded on the roadside, but none of the troops were injured. The soldiers fired several rifle shots in reply. Windows in the houses of Dr R. Wright and Miss Studdart were smashed by bullets and an occupant of one of the houses was slightly wounded.

4

DALKEY'S ATTRACTIONS

BIDDY'S COTTAGE

A traditional and authentic Irish cottage in the heart of Dalkey, it recaptures life as it used to be in Ireland, complete with a turf fire, a red dresser filled with speckled delph and a settle bed in the corner. All the old-fashioned cooking utensils are there, together with various St Bridget's crosses hanging over the doors and the dresser.

As for Biddy herself, she's Brighid McLaughlin, who was once a feature writer with the *Sunday Independent*, and who is now a noted artist and storyteller as well as a dedicated 'foodie'. She serves visitors tea and her renowned oatcakes, as well as regaling them with stories of old Dalkey and its island.

DALKEY CASTLE AND HERITAGE CENTRE

This castle, next to St Begnet's graveyard, was converted for use by the old Dalkey Town Commissioners in the 1860s. It continued as a municipal meeting place until 1998, when it became part of the new heritage centre. This centre has much material on the history of Dalkey, from medieval times to the present, and it also has a writers' gallery, with a writers' trail map and interactive screens that show all Dalkey's many literary and other cultural connections. This literary heritage also inspires a number of events in the heritage centre, including stage shows. Living history tours

Looking down Castle Street towards Dalkey Castle and heritage centre.

for schools are also popular. The centre is open daily all year, except for Tuesdays.

DALKEY'S CASTLES

A detailed map of the seven medieval castles in Dalkey can be seen at the end of Castle Street, close to the Catholic church and Archbold's Castle. This castle, together with Dalkey Castle just across the street, are the only surviving castles in Dalkey.

From the mid-fourteenth century until the late sixteenth century, ships couldn't access Dublin, as the River Liffey was silted up. So they anchored in the deep waters of Dalkey Sound. The goods were unloaded and either taken by road to the castles in Dalkey, or else they were taken on small boats directly to Ringsend.

One of the old castles, Yellow Castle, formed one of the gated entrances, while a couple of the other old castles that no longer survive, were put to other uses. In the late eighteenth

Archbold's Castle, Castle Street, Dalkey.

century, Black Castle became a butcher's premises, while Wolverton Castle, which gave its name to the present-day Ulverton Road in Dalkey, was used as a forge in the early nineteenth century.

Another of the old castles, House Castle, was demolished and the shops that now stand at numbers 24 and 25 Castle Street were built in its place.

DALKEY'S WINDMILL

Dalkey once had a windmill, close to Dalkey Avenue and the quarry, but it was short-lived. Built in 1860, it lasted until the end of the nineteenth century, but during that time it only worked for about fifteen years, pumping water up to a small reservoir at the back of Dalkey Hill, which supplied water to houses in the immediate area.

KILLINEY HILL OBELISK

The obelisk was built in 1742 on the top of Killiney Hill and from it there are spectacular views out over Dublin Bay.

It was constructed to commemorate the winter of 1740/41, which was incredibly cold and which was followed by a very wet summer. Crops failed and livestock died in the bitter weather, which was followed by another winter that was equally harsh. Icebergs floated on the River Liffey and food riots took place all over Ireland. It's considered that this forgotten famine may have killed as many as 500,000 people. Wealthy landowners organised famine-relief projects and John Malpas from Killiney Hill put up the money to build the obelisk and provide work in the area. Killiney Hill was originally called Malpas Mount after him.

Killiney Hill was acquired in 1887 as a public park, to commemorate the jubilee of Queen Victoria.

KINGS OF DALKEY

This strange and often hilarious custom dates back to the late eighteenth century.

The freemen of Dalkey were given the right in 1787 to elect the 'king', but at that stage, the tradition was already well established. The full and very lengthy title includes the King of Dalkey, the Emperor of the Muglins (the small islands close to Dalkey Island) and Baron of Bulloch. The last coronation took place on 20 August 1797 and was watched by 20,000 people. Stephen Armitage, a local pawnbroker and printer, was elected king. The ceremony didn't take place the following year, because of the 1798 Rising. A gap of 137 years followed before the ceremony was revived, in 1934. Then there was another long gap, until 1965, and the most recent time it was staged was in 1983.

DALKEY AVENUE CELTIC CROSS

This Celtic Cross is in relief, in a granite slab, that is set into the brickwork of the bridge on Dalkey Avenue. It's long been a tradition that funerals in Dalkey going to the old churchyard came up to this cross, halted and then said the Stations. Then they turned and made for the graveyard. Apparently, Martin Quinn, the son of the man who built the underground passage to Our Lady's Well, built the bridge in place of the wooden structure that formerly spanned the road. There used to be a painted cross on the old structure at which people in funeral processions did the Stations. Martin Quinn decided to replicate it in stone and he employed a local man called Farrell who carved out the cross in the granite stone.

ECHOES RETURNS TO DALKEY CASTLE AND HERITAGE CENTRE

In early October 2019, the Echoes 2019 festival returned to Dalkey Castle and Heritage Centre, with the theme of community in contemporary writing in Ireland. This festival was designed to celebrate the life and work of Maeve Binchy and other Irish writers and included thought provoking talks, walks, debates, interviews and theatrical events. Some of the personalities who took part included Gordon Snell, Chris Binchy, Carlo Gebler, Ibrahim Halawa, Róisín Ingle, Madeleine Keane, Olivia O'Leary and Lynn Ruane. Events included a Maeve Binchy and Irish writers' guided walk.

One of the themes discussed at the festival was how living on a small island affects our sense of community and how the island of Ireland influences writing and writers from Ireland, as well as the influence it has on what other countries think of Ireland. Also discussed was how writing has become a fundamental part of activism in the country, providing a voice to communities that were previously totally unheard, or at best, given little voice. The way in which all types of books, fiction, non-fiction and memories, are being used to drive social and political change in Ireland also came up for discussion.

5

HEALTH

DALKEY COMMUNITY UNIT FOR OLDER PEOPLE

This purpose-built unit, which opened in 2000, is in Dalkey village, just behind the Catholic church, and provides a wide range of services for older people.

DALKEY PRIMARY CARE TEAM

This team provided a wide range of remedial services to Dalkey residents, with some of those services available at the Dalkey Health Centre at Kilbegnet Close. The Dalkey meals on wheels service is also provided from here.

DENTISTS

Dentists in the Dalkey area include D.R.J. McCourt and Dr Hugh O'Broin, both in Castle Street, Dalkey. The Dalkey Clinic in Ulverton Road provides dental treatment and chiropractic services.

In the Killiney area, they include Fergus Cahill, Shankill Dental Clinic, Aubrey Road, Shankill, and Henry Kavanagh, Main Road, Shankill.

GPs

GPs in the Dalkey area include Dr Louis Lavelle, St Patrick's Road; Dr Maeve Kelly, Dalkey Park; Dr Eamonn Kenny, Ulverton Road and Dr Louis Lavelle, St Patrick's Road.

In the Killiney area, they include Dr Thomas Duggan, Wyattville Road, Ballybrack, Dr Michael Houlihan of Bayview Drive, Killiney and the Shankill family practice, Shankill.

DALKEY LODGE NURSING HOME

This twenty-eight bed facility closed in 2017, because of the cost of improvements that would have been needed for improvements to meet health service standards.

The nursing home, which had many residents who had lived in Dalkey all their lives, had been open for nearly thirty years.

GROVE NURSING HOME

The house was built in 1840 and was acquired in 1925 by James O'Mara, a TD. He died in 1948 and after his death, his widow, Agnes, and their unmarried son, Stephen, continued to live in the house until Agnes' death in 1958. The family sold the house soon afterwards and in 1980, it opened as a thirty-two-bed nursing home. However, by 2019, the nursing home was closed and up for sale, with a price tag of €4.5 million.

KILLINEY GROVE NURSING HOME

This nursing home, owned by the Silver Stream Healthcare group, is at Killiney Hill Road and began in 1999. The director of nursing is Tania Spelman.

OUR LADY'S MANOR, DALKEY

Our Lady's Manor is probably the best-known nursing home in the area. Situated at Ulverton Road, Dalkey, near to Bulloch Castle and harbour, it is run under the Carmelite not-for-profit health system and can cater for up to 118 residents, on three floors. It has a wide range of facilities for its residents, who are also encouraged to go to Dalkey village, including local pubs, as well as for local walks. Official health inspections have consistently found that Our Lady's Manor is maintained to a good standard.

OTHER CLINICS AND HEALTH SERVICES

Local services include: Ross Allen, physiotherapy and chiropractic clinic, Castle Street; John Callaghan and Rachel Henderson, natural healing, Castle Street; Dalkey Beauty and Active Balance Clinic, Castle Street; Helen Foley, reflexologist, Castle Street; Paul Gill, optician, St Patrick's Road; John Hanrahan, medical herbalist and nutritional therapist, Sarah Hanrahan, Grace Kinirons and Gillian McIlroy, all at 21 Church Road; Carolyn Sinnott, meditation and relaxation classes, Castle Street; South Dublin Physiotherapy and chiropractic clinic, Castle Stree and Thai Yoi Therapy Centre, Castle Street.

SUE RYDER HOUSE

At Carrig na Greine, Coliemore Road, Dalkey, the Sue Ryder Foundation provides a wide range of care services for residents with disabilities, who live in around fifty units of accommodation, bungalows and apartments. Retired people in the area can also take part in activities such as aerobics and walking.

When the site was bought from the Loreto nuns, over twenty years ago, it included Carrig na Greine, an early eighteenth-century mansion. An enormous amount of work was carried out on the house to provide accommodation for residents of the Sue Ryder home.

6

MODERN HOUSES

BARTRA CAPITAL HIT BY PLANNING DELAYS IN DALKEY

Bartra Capital, led by Richard Barrett, which is developing many housing schemes in the Dublin area, has met with many planning delays to its proposed scheme at Bulloch Harbour, Dalkey, as of 2019.

In 2014, a one-bedroom house at Bartra Tower, Harbour Road, Dalkey, was up for sale for €1 million and at the time, was described as the most expensive one-bedroom home in Ireland.

DALKEY DEVELOPMENT OPPOSED

In the summer of 2018, Ann-Marie Lucey and Denis Lucey of Castle Court, Dalkey, were given permission to challenge the development of fifty apartments, three and four storeys high, on part of the Castle Park school lands, with which they shared an entrance.

DALKEY HOUSE FOR SALE

Number 5, Saval Park Road, Dalkey, a semi-detached house with five bedrooms, went up for sale in 2019 for €1,250,000. At the same time, The Flags, a modern four-bedroomed bungalow with a vast lawn, was up for sale for €1,450,000. Also in 2019, a detached house, Scopello, on Ulverton Road, Dalkey, described as being so modern it was like a spaceship, was on the market for €1,795,000.

GORSE HILL, KILLINEY

Few local homes have raised as much legal controversy in the area as Gorse Hill, where Brian and Mary Pat O'Donnell built an enormous house that extended to 1,000m^2 and had six bedrooms and seven bathrooms. One local legal expert described it as a 'bog standard house', which must qualify as the understatement of the decade as far as Killiney houses are concerned.

The trouble is that the O'Donnells were declared bankrupt in 2013, with debts of €71 million. However, in November 2018, the couple downsized to a €1.8 million house, Laragh House, on Killiney Avenue. Their new home had decor designed by their eldest daughter, Blaise, who wanted to recreate some of the features of the old house at Gorse Hill.

KILLINEY HOUSE FOR SALE

A modern two-storey house at Avondale Road in Killiney was put on the market in 2019 for €700,000, considered to be a very reasonable price. In contrast, a luxurious penthouse apartment with panoramic views, in a gated development at Killiney Hill Park, was for sale for €1,395,000.

MODERN KILLINEY HOUSE FOR SALE FOR NEARLY €2 MILLION

Rock Lodge House, a stunning modern house with four bedrooms on Claremont Road, close to Killiney village, was put up for sale in 2019 for €1,925,000. Its facilities include a home cinema and a snooker room. At about the same time, a modern detached bungalow at Cenacle Grove, a private enclave in Killiney, was for sale for €1,375,000.

SAN ELMO LODGE, TORCA ROAD, KILLINEY

Perhaps the most notable modern house in the area and certainly the most lauded, this two-storey glass-box-style house was designed by Tom de Paor. It was built in 2007 and has 353m^2 of space on two floors. The gardens are extensive, running to about 1,600m^2. It overlooks Killiney Bay. The building was originally known as House V and replaced an older house that had been the gate lodge for San Elmo, constructed in 1870 further along the Vico Road.

The first owners of the new house only lived there for a few months, before they relocated to central Europe, and it sold for €6 million. The house remains as iconic as ever; it hasn't dated at all. In June 2019, it was put back on the market, for just over €4.6 million.

7

NATURAL HISTORY

BULLOCH HARBOUR

Built 200 years ago, the harbour used to be noted for its use by local fishermen, although their boats have long since vanished. Its coal yards were used for imported coal and these were later replaced by boatyards, which have also disappeared.

Construction of the harbour began in the winter of 1818/19 and was carried out by the Dublin Ballast Board, which is now the Dublin Port Company. During Storm Emma in 2018, Bulloch Harbour was badly damaged, as many of the granite blocks were knocked out of place.

These days, the harbour is used mainly by private boat owners, although the design of the harbour, as well as the impact of tides and bad weather, can all combine to make it a difficult place to navigate.

Despite all the ups and downs of Bulloch Harbour, its bicentenary commemorations got great local support and created much interest.

Bulloch Harbour still has a strong place in the affections of local people. A couple of years ago, a property development company called Bartra Capital proposed a mixed use development of commercial and residential units, right on the seafront at Bulloch Harbour. The proposal unleashed a barrage of hostile public opinion. One well-known objector to the scheme was local resident Christy Moore, a noted folk singer, who said the proposed development had the potential to damage the amenity value of the area for sailing, swimming, fishing, walking and regular recreation, as well as posing concerns for wildlife and the ecosystem.

Planning permission for the development was refused and the developer submitted a revised plan, which was approved, but at the time of writing local protestors are still absolutely determined to prevent any new developments they consider unwarranted for the Bulloch Harbour area.

Bulloch Harbour.

Bulloch Harbour.

Bulloch Harbour.

THE CAT'S LADDER

From the Vico Road, a steep climb leads up to Dalkey Hill, via some stone steps known locally as The Cat's Ladder.

CONGER EEL IN DALKEY

Way back in August 1915, the capture of an enormous conger eel off the coast of Dalkey created huge excitement in the village.

The conger eel was described as being of huge dimensions and was caught by a well-known local angler, Willie Flanagan. He had set out for an evening's fishing with three friends, Ned Carroll, Mick Flanagan and Pat McBride. It was said at the time that the denizens of the finny deep had a rough time at the hands of, or rather the hooks of, this distinguished quartet of anglers. Several fine specimens of the square-nosed turbot fell to Pat McBride's fishing hook, while Mick Flanagan landed some splendid mackerel and also several good specimens of rock bream. Ned Carroll didn't fare so well, as his line got entangled in the boat, which he nearly turned over by pulling it in. After a hard struggle, he landed a seagull, but apart from landing a small whiting, he had no success that evening.

It was coming close to nightfall when Willie Flanagan felt a severe tug on his line and was nearly pulled out of the boat. However, he held on with grim determination and very shortly, a huge conger eel raised its head above the waters before returning swiftly to the deeps of Dalkey Sound. The boat was being pulled here and there by the giant fish, whose tactics evoked much admiration from the crowd on the beach, who were following the fishing events with great enthusiasm. At length, Ned Carroll took a pair of tongs that they had on the boat and grasped the conger eel, dragging as much of it as he could into the boat.

In the confrontation with the fish, the anglers lost one of the oars from the boat, but Mick Flanagan used the tongs to row ashore. The eel, which measured very nearly 6m long, was drawn up on the beach, at the end of an unexpected dramatic fishing expedition off Dalkey.

DALKEY ISLAND

Dalkey Island, which is reached by boat from Coliemore Harbour, is quite small, extending to just 9 hectares, but it has a profusion of wildlife, helped by the fact that the island hasn't been inhabited for the past 200 years. If the weather is fine, a boat trip out to the island makes for a pleasant half day, or longer, excursion.

The island has long had its own herd of wild goats, as well as black rabbits. Many of Ireland's breeding and coastal birds, such as cormorants, mallards and razorbills nest on the island. Many migratory species, such as Brent geese and swallows, often use it as a resting spot. Offshore, the waters around the island are rich in fish, such as coalfish, mackerel and pollock. There is also has a colony of seals, which has expanded considerably in recent years.

The island holds the ruins of two churches, one dating from the seventh century, the other from the ninth. The older

Coliemore Harbour, Dalkey, with the Muglins in the distance.

Dalkey Island, complete with its Martello tower.

church was named after St Begnet. In the early nineteenth century, a Martello tower was also built on the island and is still structurally intact.

Just to the east of Dalkey Island are a group of rocks, known as The Muglins, which have a warning beacon for shipping.

DALKEY QUARRY

Dalkey quarry was abandoned for quarrying after much granite was dug out in the early nineteenth century to build the new harbour at what was then Kingstown, now Dún Laoghaire. Granite was also dug out for the building of the South Bull Wall, at the entrance to Dublin port and for paving the streets of Dublin. In the 1840s, granite from the Dalkey quarry was exported to build a new cathedral in St John's, Newfoundland.

In 1914, most of the land at the quarry was added to the existing Killiney Hill Park, and it was all opened up to the public. Much later, in 1998, the local council proposed to turn the west valley in the disused quarry into a caravan halting site for travellers, but this plan met with such strong opposition from local residents and others that it was eventually scrapped. Since then, apart from a path and some steps, the old quarry has been left wild. All the vegetation is home to wildlife, including foxes, while in recent years, peregrine falcons have been nesting in the cliffs.

Today, the main attraction for the old quarry is for climbers, and it has become one of the most popular rock-climbing locations in Ireland. There are over 350 routes and some of these are among the hardest single pitch rock climbs in Ireland. The quarry routes are almost all single pitch, between 10m and 35m in length, and in keeping with local rock-climbing traditions, there are no bolts on any of the climbs in the quarry.

KILLINEY

Killiney is a very attractive residential area, with south-facing slopes facing Killiney Bay, with Bray Head in the distance. Many of the houses were built during the nineteenth century, which means that they have very mature gardens with many shrubs and trees.

KILLINEY BEACH

In March 2019, Killiney beach, which is made up of rock and pebbles, was covered in sand, a most unusual sight. In previous instances of the beach being partly covered with sand, small sections of wet sand could be seen during periods of low tide, but the 2019 covering of sand was spread right across the beach for the first time in years.

KILLINEY HILL PARK

First opened to the public in 1887, its initial name was Victoria Park. The land for the park was purchased by the Queen Victoria Memorial Association, to commemorate the Queen's golden jubilee, from Robert Warren junior, for £5,000. The park was opened by Prince Albert and it has remained a public park up to the present day. The old Dún Laoghaire corporation increased the size of the park in the late 1930s by buying the rest of Dalkey Hill and the lands at Burmah Road, which brought its size up to 80 hectares. This extension included the considerable area of the old Dalkey Quarry. At the time, the corporation tried to buy Mount Eagle, so that the park could be extended at Vico Road, but it was outbid at auction by a private buyer, Con Smith.

The Vico Fields, the wild land above the railway line at White Rock, had been bought by the corporation in 1926, to prevent any further building. Surprisingly, many new apartment developments have been built in the immediate area during the past three decades.

OLD MARINE BIOLOGY STATION, COLIEMORE HARBOUR

University College Dublin (UCD) used to have a marine biology station at Coliemore Harbour in Dalkey, where students could come to study marine life on and around the Dalkey coastline. The deep waters of Dalkey Sound, the sandbanks beyond Sorrento Point and the rocky foreshore made for ideal conditions for the students, where they could study lichen, flowering plants and seaweeds, as well as crustacea, fish and molluscs. The old marine biology station is now the clubhouse for Dalkey Rowing Club.

OLD SECOND WORLD WAR EMERGENCY SIGN RESTORED

During the Second World War Emergency, between 1939 and 1945, many signs were built around the country to warn international aircrews that they were flying over Ireland,

Coliemore Harbour, Dalkey.

Coliemore Harbour, Dalkey.

which stayed neutral. Most of those eighty-three signs have long since been lost, but a sign marked 'Eire 7' was found at Hawk's Cliff in Dalkey. It's just off the Vico Road, down a path that leads to the sea and across a pedestrian bridge over the railway line.

The size of the sign is quite big, about 30m x 10m, and it was restored to its original state, in 2019, by the Dalkey Tidy Towns group. There's also another relic in Dalkey of the Second World War, a lookout position on the summit of Sorrento Park.

RIGHTS OF WAY

Dalkey has an astonishing number of rights of way, twenty-six in all, which embrace all areas of the town, from the foreshore to inland parts. Among the most interesting is the one from Bulloch Harbour along the foreshore, while another runs from Loreto Avenue to Lady's Well, also on the foreshore.

8

OLD HOUSES

ABBEY LEA, KILLINEY

This house, which is the official residence of the Australian Ambassador in Dublin, is comparatively new, an Arts and Crafts-style house that was built in 1909, when it was called Marino, a rebuilding of an earlier house on the site.

It was built by Laurence Waldron, who had been an Irish Parliamentary Party MP for the St Stephen's Green constituency in Dublin, from 1904 to 1910. When the Seanad was established in Dublin under the 1920 Home Rule Bill, he was elected, but resigned before its first meeting. He was an avid book collector.

Waldron died at Marino on 27 December 1923. Just over forty years ago, in 1964, it was bought by the Australian government for £18,000.

ALVERNO HOUSE, DALKEY

Standing at the corner of Sorrento Road and Vico Road, this vast Gothic pile was built in the late nineteenth century. Its richly decorated interior includes stained-glass windows and a huge glazed dome at the top of the staircase. In 1993, it was bought for £1.5 million by Alphonsus O'Mara, a door manufacturer, and his wife, Claudia. By 2017, the house was up for sale for €8.5 million, although a year later, the price dropped to €7.5 million.

ARD NA GREINE, ARDEEVIN ROAD, DALKEY

This beautifully decorated family home, on the grand scale, dates back to the later nineteenth century. The two upper floors have a total of six bedrooms, while the family room on the ground floor has access to the vast garden covering most of the 0.2 hectares of the site. The south-facing lawns have sea views, while access to the house is by a driveway that's lined with hedges and shrubs.

When the house went up for sale in 2018, the price tag was appropriately high: €2,450,000.

ATLANTA, DALKEY

Atlanta, one of a pair of houses built at Coliemore Road in 1870, was once the home of Theodora FitzGibbon, the food critic, and her husband George Morrison, a film director. When they lived there, they shared the house with the then owner, Aileen Hamilton.

In 1987, Vincent Browne, a former newspaper editor and TV presenter, and his wife Jean, bought the house for £94,000. By 2010, the house had got far too big for them, as their two daughters had grown up. They also needed money for a new, smaller home and a pension. At that stage, Mr Browne's debts were estimated to have been €1.5 million. They got €3.25 million for the three-storey house, with wonderful views from its back garden of Dalkey Island.

AYESHA CASTLE, KILLINEY

Out of all the big houses in the Killiney area, this one has the most dramatic setting. It was built in the mid-nineteenth century by Robert Warren, a noted local developer of the time. It's in the style of a pseudo Norman castle and was built on the side of a hill, giving wonderful views over Killiney Bay, towards Bray Head and the Wicklow Mountains. Built from locally quarried granite, the house is square in plan, with a projecting block and also a circular tower. With its many battlements and crenellations, it looks most impressive.

In the late 1920s, the castle was gutted by fire, but the ruin was bought by Sir Thomas Talbot Power, then owner of Power's Distillery in Dublin. He used his vast wealth to restore the castle; new features included an impressive new hall and a dining room, both oak panelled. In 1930, he renamed the restored castle Ayesha, after a fictional goddess in Ryder Haggard's book, *She*. In 1996 the castle was bought for over £2 million by Enya, the singer-songwriter renowned for her reclusiveness. She has remained resident in Ayesha Castle ever since.

BARTRA HOUSE, HARBOUR ROAD, DALKEY

This enormous detached house by the sea stands on Harbour Road, near Bulloch Harbour in Dalkey. It's on 0.8 hectares of land while the house itself extends to 1,025m², making it an enormous pile. The house was built in the mid-1850s and was originally known as Bartra Hall. One of its earliest residents was Robert Booth, who founded the Dunlop tyre factory in Dublin in 1891. He had also lived at Victoria House on Coliemore Road in Dalkey before moving to Bartra House around 1900. Coming much closer to the present, the house was owned during the 1970s by Kevin Anderson, father of the eponymously named Kevin Anderson, a cinema mogul. He developed an unusual 1970s house, The Fairways, and two smaller coach house style developments. Anderson sold the house and its land in 1981 to Noel Stephenson, an insurance broker, and his wife, Helen, for IR£500,000. Noel was the brother of controversial architect Sam Stephenson, who was responsible for designing such buildings as the old Central Bank of Ireland in Dame Street. When the Stephensons took over Bartra House, it occupied twice as much land as at present, but the house was half the size of the present dwelling. Beside the house was a gatehouse, while also on the land was a Martello tower. While the Stephensons owned Bartra House, a number of developments took place. A large apartment block, Bartra Rock, and a detached house, Bartra Cove, were built on the site. In 1996, the Stephensons sold Bartra House for what was then a record, IR£1.95 million, and moved next door to Bartra Cove, a very modern house designed by the Stephensons' architect daughter, Simone. Bartra House itself was sold to Gavin O'Reilly, who later became chief executive of Independent News & Media, then owned by his father, Sir Anthony O'Reilly. Gavin O'Reilly and his then wife, actress Alison Doody, moved into Bartra House. While they didn't carry out any more developments on the lands surrounding the house, by the time they sold it in 2012, the house had been doubled in size, twice as big as it was during Kevin Anderson's ownership.

During 2012, the price tag for Bartra House was reduced from €3.9 million to €3 million, before it was sold to Colm Delves, the CEO of a Caribbean-based telecoms company owned by Denis O'Brien, who was also the arch- enemy of the O'Reillys at Independent News & Media, which O'Brien eventually came to control, before the company was sold on again in 2019.

While the Delves family occupied Bartra House, many more changes were made to Bartra House. The basement, which had been used for staff accommodation, was turned into an entertainment centre, with a large cinema, a pool room and gym. The ground floor reception rooms were returned to their former glory and a large open-plan kitchen was built.

BELLEVUE PARK, KILLINEY

This fine house, on the western side of Killiney, is now occupied by the St Joseph of Cluny convent and school. The house was once at the centre of a large estate so big that it extended as far as Killiney. Bellevue House is a large, square house with an Ionic portico. Its most unusual feature is the circular hall. Six curved doors in the hall lead to the main rooms, and also to the staircase, which is a cantilevered stone structure of great elegance. Architectural historian Peter Pearson notes that what is now the convent chapel was once a lavish Italianate style billiard room, built by the Anketell Jones family, who owned Bellevue House until 1896.

BEULAH HOUSE, HARBOUR ROAD, DALKEY

One of the finest seaside residences in the area, it dates from the earlier nineteenth century, when Harbour Road in Dalkey was called Ballast Office Road. Currently, the house is set on three levels, including a basement, and has a floor space of $560m^2$, on a site of about 0.6 hectares. The house has several reception rooms on the ground floor, along with five bedrooms and three bathrooms upstairs. Close to the main house is Beulah Court, a gated development of six detached houses, all built on the lands of Beulah Court.

While the house is certainly one of the finest in the Dalkey area, its grounds are unusual, because they slope gently down towards the sea, so that almost all of the land is usable, a contrast to the beautiful but much more difficult terrains of houses on the Vico Road.

Despite all the recent extensions built in the gardens, there's still plenty of room for even further building or extensions to the main house.

When the house was sold in 1979 for IR£379,000, it was an astonishing price for a house in the Dublin area. Yet when it came back to the market in 2015, the price tag was €6.5 million.

BULLOCH CASTLE, DALKEY

This castle, standing on high ground overlooking Bulloch Harbour, was built in medieval times by the Cisterican monks of St Mary's Abbey to protect their fisheries at Dalkey. It's the best-preserved medieval building in south Co. Dublin.

One of its features is the spiral staircase that heads from the ground floor, with its vaulted undercroft, to the main hall above. The castle was restored in the 1960s by the Carmelite Sisters for the Aged and the Infirm and today, the castle, close to Loreto Abbey school, remains in good structural condition, although it's not open to the public.

In the early eighteenth century, a three-storey gable-ended house was added to the north-east corner of the castle, while a row of cottages backed onto the nearby road. This house was enlarged in Victorian times, but eventually, it was demolished in the 1980s. What were once the gardens of Bulloch Castle extended southwards but all that land is now occupied by the building of Our Lady's Manor, which caters for elderly residents. It opened in 1965 as a 100-bedroom block and since then, various large extensions have been built, which completely dominate Bulloch Harbour.

During the 1830s, Alderman Perrin had a group of four cottages built near a steep hill, known as Castle Steps, which is behind Our Lady's Manor, for the workmen he employed at Bulloch Castle and their families. In the early part of the nineteenth century, a total of ten pilots' cottages were built on the quayside at Bulloch Harbour for the pilots working out of the harbour and their families but the original outline of those cottages has long since disappeared.

CAERLEON, CHURCH ROAD, KILLINEY

This house, which faces Church Road in Killiney, was built in the late 1880s for Frederick Toutan, a wine merchant. In much more recent times, it used to be a nursing home called the Kylemore Clinic, so ever since, the house has been known as Kylemore. The house has a most unusual feature, an arched corner loggia and terrace, built into a rear corner of the house, and giving access to the gardens.

Close on thirty years ago, extensive archaeological excavations were carried out in the grounds of the house. One of the discoveries was an early medieval graveyard in which about 1,500 bodies were buried. Also near to the house were the remains of the earliest church in Killiney, built before about 1120. The 'kill' word, derived from Irish, is usually taken to mean a church, and the name of Killiney is derived from this ancient church.

CASTLE PARK, DALKEY

Back in the 1860s, the Ordnance Survey maps of the time showed that the lands between Dalkey and Sandycove were still largely undeveloped. The area also had many small quarries. But one house did stand out, Castle Park, previously known as Castle Perrin.

The original house was built in the 1820s, in late Georgian style. By 1830, it was owned by Alderman Arthur Perrin, who lived in nearby Bulloch Castle. He rented out Castle Perrin to wealthy members of the British administration in Dublin Castle. Perrin also had the house enlarged by turning it into a mock Tudor mansion, complete with a battlemented tower. Inside the house, the impressive feature is a large hall, with an arcade, designed in the Tudor style. All the rooms have elaborate plasterwork cornices and centrepieces.

After Perrin's time owning the house, it was occupied by various legal personalities during the latter part of the nineteenth century. In 1904, Castle Park School was started here by W.P. Toone and, in its earlier years, had many pupils from England and elsewhere outside Ireland. Today, the school is still going strong and it is still surrounded by a magnificent stretch of open space, with many trees, as well as a fine garden. The entrance on Castle Park Road is distinguished by a grandiose, castellated entrance, complete with archway and circular towers.

CLIFF CASTLE, DALKEY

One of Dalkey's most distinctive residences, it stands on about 0.4 hectares of land and has Italianate gardens running down to the sea and its own private harbour.

It was built about 1840 as a summer residence, and was converted into a twenty-bedroom hotel in the 1920s by the Murphy family. Neighbours often complained about the noise from dances at the hotel and from people driving in and out of the hotel at night. These complaints culminated in a court case in 1936. A quieter crowd often met at the hotel, however, the Dalkey Literary and Historical Society.

In 1946, a floating mine exploded close to the back of the hotel, causing serious damage to both it and the neighbouring houses.

In the mid-1960s, the Murphys sold the hotel and moved to the Bel-Air Hotel in Ashford, Co. Wicklow, which they had bought prior to selling the Cliff Castle Hotel. Timothy Murphy died in 1970 and his wife Bridie in 1981.

1971 saw the Cliff Castle up for sale again, when it was bought for £70,000 by Jack Kirwan, owner of the nearby Colamore Hotel, since demolished and replaced by the Coliemore Road apartment development.

One of Jack Kirwan's innovations at the Cliff Castle Hotel was the Fingers disco, which stayed open until 2 a.m. nightly. In 1978, the hotel was sold again and the new owners introduced a Polynesian-style nightclub called the Coral Reef. By the late 1980s, the Cliff Castle had reverted to being a private residence. In the early years of this century, it was rented by the Moroccan embassy as a residence for its ambassador.

CLIFF HOUSE, KILLINEY
HILL ROAD, KILLINEY

Cliff House, which stands on 0.6 hectares of land and has 1,450m^2 of accommodation, has a rare distinction in Killiney – it's the largest house in the area.

It dates back to the early 1860s, when it was designed by one of the most prominent architects of the time, Benjamin Woodward of the Deane and Woodward practice. Among their many other designs was the Kildare Street Club in Dublin city centre, close to Trinity College, now occupied by the Alliance Française. Woodward died half way through the construction of Cliff House, so his work was completed by his partner, Sir Thomas Newenham Deane. At the same time that Cliff House was designed, the practice also created several other neighbouring houses, Fernside, Illerton (now The Neale/Alloa), Palermo and South Hill.

Cliff House was originally known as Green Hill, and was built for an opera singer called Joseph Robinson. The name wasn't changed to Cliff House until the 1920s. Then followed a series of owners. Richard Meredith bought it in 1931 and his family lived there until 1945, when it was sold again to Arthur Rashleigh, who lived in the house until his death in 1953. It remained in the occupancy of his widow, Edith, for another decade.

Then, in 1963, Cliff House was bought by Harold Spiro, who owned the Imco dry cleaning business, noted for its Art Deco headquarters on the Merrion Road, Booterstown, and demolished in 1974 and replaced by a most unimaginative office block. His wife Elvina Iris was an avid bridge player. When the Spiros owned Cliff House, they built an unattractive two-storey flat-roofed extension onto the side of Cliff House.

Eventually, the Spiros moved to Spain and they sold Cliff House in 1970. It was sold again in 1974 to James and Dorothy Pugh, who owned Cliff House until Dorothy's death in 1985. The next owners, who bought the house in 1986, were a German couple. Peter Schmidt was a German businessman very involved in the ship repair business, and his wife was Loreta. Schmidt's business operations were based in Dublin and Dubai and he paid IR£160,000 after auction for the house.

The Schmidts didn't always lived there and during their absences, they rented out the house. Among the showbiz people who rented Cliff House was Mel Gibson, while he was in Ireland to film *Braveheart*, and the rock band Simple Minds. Eventually, the Schmidts sold the house, which was bought in 1996 for IR£900,000 from Peter Schmidt by Charlie Burchill of Simple Minds. While he was there, the house was occupied for a time by fellow band member Jim Kerr, who also lived just across the road, in Killiney House, with his then wife, Patsy Kensit.

When the Burchills took over Cliff House, they carried out extensive restoration work in 1998, doing away with all the original plasterwork above basement level. They decorated the house in French and Moroccan themes and the reception rooms were given a Louis XV style makeover.

The Burchills put the house on the market in 2004, when it was bought for €5.3 million by a solicitor turned hedge fund adviser. He extended the house to its present size and he also removed the non-original extensions. Today, it's a very impressive house, with four large reception rooms, an orangery and kitchen, six bedrooms and four bathrooms. At garden level, the house has a huge indoor swimming pool, a sauna, a gym and a billiard room. Outside, the grounds have a large area for parking cars, as well as perfectly landscaped grounds that run down to Strathmore Road, where there is pedestrian access.

COASTGUARD STATION COTTAGES, DALKEY

Beside the coastguard station, on nearby Beacon Hill, five cottages were built in the 1840s for the personnel who manned the station, and their families. In the old days, the cottages included a lookout tower, a laundry and a well. A report published in 1824 had recommended that an eight-person coastguard station should be built at Dalkey. That report also noted that smuggling onto the beaches of Killiney Bay was carried out quite frequently by pilot boats.

DALKEY LODGE, BARNHILL ROAD, DALKEY

Located on Barnhill Road, just to the west of Castle Street in Dalkey, Dalkey Lodge is the oldest house in the area, described as long ago as 1768 as a 'neat house'. The man who made that description was Peter Wilson, who in the late eighteenth century published an annual directory called Wilson's Almanack. One of his numerous accounts was of what he found in Dalkey, including the excellent view from Dalkey Lodge, across Dublin Bay to the new lighthouse on the Hill of Howth, which he said was skirted in summer with a mixture of delightful spots of corn and other plants and flowers.

As for Dalkey Lodge, it was built as a large three-storey house, five windows wide, with a fine cut stone doorcase that had been created in the mid-eighteenth century. Later on, a number of additions were made to the side and the back of the house. In the Victorian era, the house was owned by Thomas Henry, who had a sundial installed in the garden, bearing the inscription 'Dalkey Lodge AD 1869'. A quarry that once stood beside the house was filled in and eventually, a small housing estate was built on the site, named Old Quarry. Barnhill Road was and still is, one of the principal roads leading into the centre of Dalkey, so 200 years ago, it was an ideal place for a farrier's workshop. The remains of an old forge can be seen in the horseshoe shaped entrance, long since blocked up, at Dalkey Lodge.

At the time that Dalkey Lodge got its sundial in 1869, one of the most colourful books ever produced about Dalkey was published, *Irish Varieties* by James J. Gaskin. He observed the great changes wrought in Dalkey from 1840 onwards, heightened by the arrival of the railway in 1844; Dalkey was changed completely from a small, isolated village surrounded by fields. It became a town in its own right, complete with its own local administration, and many fine houses and terraces were built on the rocky terrain. Architectural historian Peter Pearson notes that Dalkey has a greater diversity of house types than Killiney, with many more cottages, as well as small villas and terraces. Dalkey gardens are generally smaller than those in Killiney. But as Dalkey celebrated such expansion in the thirty years from 1840, one house had already been there for a century, Dalkey Lodge.

INNISCORRIG, DALKEY

This impressive house was built in 1847 on the coast road at Dalkey, in a medieval style, at a time when the great famine was at its worst. Initially, the house was a square, stone-built mansion, with prominent chimneys. Later on, the size of the house was doubled by the addition of several more enormous rooms, as well as an enormous conservatory and a short tower.

The house was built for a well-known Dublin physician, Sir Dominic Corrigan, who moved from Merrion Square to Dalkey. One of Corrigan's concerns was the poor quality of drinking water available for the poorest classes in the city and he was one of the staunchest campaigners for the creation of the water supply from the Vartry reservoir at Roundwood in Co. Wicklow in the 1860s. He also wanted to ensure that a proper water supply was available for fire-fighting purposes. Corrigan also had a four-year tenure as a Westminster MP, from 1870 to 1874. He was highly respected in his lifetime and he is buried at St Andrew's church in Westland Row, Dublin.

But one thing Corrigan was short of was modesty; he had a bust of himself placed over the front door at Inniscorrig. Corrigan also had the largest private harbour built on the Dalkey coastline. One distinguished visitor to the house was King Edward VII, who was king of what was the United Kingdom of Great Britain and Ireland from 1901 until 1910. That royal visit was commemorated by a crown and a star set in pebbles on either side of the main entrance door, a decorative feature that can still be seen today.

KENAH HILL, KILLINEY

Kenah Hill is a large Italianate-style house at the top of Killiney Hill, where it is surrounded by Scots pine trees. Built in the mid-nineteenth century, it has appropriately grandiose features such as the decorative mouldings around its doors and windows. The main elevation is six bays wide and two storeys high. Before its present name, the house had two other names, Frankfort and Stoneleigh. About two decades ago, the house was completely renovated and it was also separated from its stableyard which itself has distinguishing features such as a cupola and a copper dome.

KHYBER PASS, DALKEY

This great Victorian house once stood on a great height overlooking the railway line at Dalkey, with magnificent views across both Dublin and Killiney bays

The house was built in the mid-nineteenth century and was originally a two-storey structure over basement, a most imposing mansion. It was built by James Milo Burke, who lived there for about thirty years, until 1880, when he moved to the adjacent Queenstown Castle, overlooking Dalkey Sound.

In the late nineteenth century, the house was much expanded, with the addition of a completely new front, which included two-storeyed bay windows and an elaborate canopied entrance with a mosaic floor. The new exterior was treated in the Italian style, including an attractive cornice.

During the later nineteenth century, the great Irish nationalist leader, Charles Stewart Parnell, lived in the house. A subsequent occupier was Bryan Cooper, a noted Unionist politician, who became a Unionist MP for South County Dublin in 1910. He was one of the few Unionist politicians in this part of Ireland who remained in politics after partition and he was elected to the Dáil in 1923 as an independent. The Cooper family kept the Khyber Pass house until 1926, when it was sold to a local builder and developer.

In time, the great house was converted into the Khyber House Hotel, which closed down in1980. It stood derelict until 1986, when it was demolished. But long before that demolition, as the hotel's fortunes waned, blocks of apartments were built in its grounds, despite widespread local opposition.

KILLINEY BEACH

Killiney beach has long been a favourite bathing place in the locality and as early as 1757, a map of the district showed a bathhouse near White Rock. Peter Pearson notes that the old tearooms on the beach were a more modern relic of bathing and boating on the beach. Up until the 1950s, the structure was used as a dance pavilion and as tea rooms. It was also possible, in the old days, to hire boats at what is called locally the White Cottage, a good description for the Greek-style tea rooms.

Close to Killiney beach are a remarkable pair of semi-detached, stone houses built in Victorian times. They were designed by George Wilkinson, who also designed many railway stations and workhouses in Ireland. These houses at Killiney were built from granite and include such features as battlemented towers. The houses, together with the Martello tower, which has been converted to residential use, overlook the sand and shingle of the beach at the point where the Loughlinstown River flows into the sea.

George Wilkinson also designed another fine house in the locality, Temple Hill, an impressive Victorian house with a temple in its grounds. For the past thirty years, it has been the family home of Bono, U2's lead singer.

KILLINEY HILL ROAD

This steep road was the only north–south thoroughfare in Killiney until the Vico Road was extended in the

View from the top of Killiney Hill Road, Killiney.

mid-nineteenth century. Following that, a whole network of roads was built in Killiney, opening up an explosion of house building that lasted for the second half of the nineteenth century.

KILLINEY HOUSE, KILLINEY

In 1994, Jim Kerr, the lead singer of Simple Minds, and his wife Patsy Kensit bought this double-fronted, late-Victorian house, complete with eighteenth-century coach houses. The Kerrs sold it in 1999 for the equivalent of €3.8 million, doubling their original investment. The purchaser was a telecoms entrepreneur, Michael Maye, and when he sold it on after a six-year restoration programme he put the €9 million he got into his villa on the Bay of Monaco.

LARAGH HOUSE, KILLINEY

This large late-Victorian mansion, just off Killiney Avenue in Killiney, has a wealth of history hidden within its walls.

When the house was built, it was set within a vast estate, but much of the land was sold off around forty years ago for a discreet cul-de-sac of much smaller, more modern homes. These days, the house has 0.4 hectares of garden attached, but it still has a sweeping driveway that can take lots of cars. There's also a range of terraced lawns and patios, which at the lowest level are flat enough for badminton, croquet or tennis. The gardens also have a small summer house.

Within the house itself, which runs to nearly 650m², there are several very gracious reception rooms, complete with ornate wallpaper, high ceilings, bay windows and lots of original decorative features. The ground floor features include a pair of beautiful formal rooms, a music room, a study and a dining room. But in many ways, the real highlight of the ground floor is the Dalkey Design kitchen, which is big enough to have dining and living spaces.

Upstairs, the house has five bedrooms, all well sized. The master bedroom has a fine bay window, is en suite and has a private balcony terrace. For many years, only the two upper floors of the house were lived in and the basement was filled with rubble. In recent years, the whole basement area has been cleared out and converted into extra living space, while beside the main house, a former coach house has been converted into a two-bedroomed mews.

Earlier in the twentieth century, the house had two very interesting occupiers. The first was John Hughes, a political associate of Eamon de Valera, who became not only a long-serving Taoiseach, but subsequently a president of Ireland. In the late 1920s, when de Valera was making strenuous efforts to set up the *Irish Press* newspaper (launched in 1931), Hughes invested what was then the grand sum of £200. While the *Irish Press* was initially successful as a morning newspaper and spawned both the *Evening Press* and the *Sunday Press*, the *Irish Press* group was to collapse sixty-five years later.

After Hughes' occupancy of the house, an even more daring entrepreneur bought Laragh House. Joe 'Spud' Murphy was an inveterate inventor always seeking new ways of making money. Immediately after the Second World War, the biro was invented and Murphy was quick to seize the rights to sell it in Ireland. He also brought a newly created fruit drink called Ribena to Irish consumers, but his really big deal was setting up Tayto crisps in the early 1950s. The firm started in a small way, just off Moore Street in central Dublin, where half a dozen workers fried and boxed potato crisps. The big breakthrough for the firm came with its invention of cheese and onion flavoured crisps. 'Spud' Murphy became extremely wealthy on the back of his potato crisps and his purchase of Laragh House was just one of his extravagant personal investments. He also had an enormous collection of cashmere sweaters, but the most ostentatious symbol of his wealth was his Rolls-Royce. This was traded in every two years for a new model and Murphy used to love driving around both Dublin and London in his Rolls-Royce, 'flashing' his cash.

MONTEROSA, DALKEY

This fine Colonial-style residence, which was built about 1860, stands on a prime corner site where Sorrento Road meets Sorrento Close. It's halfway between the Vico Road and Dalkey's centre.

The three-storey house has fine sea views from its upper floors. In 2019, it was put up for sale for close on €3 million.

MOUNT EAGLE, KILLINEY

Set in a dramatic location on the Killiney coastline, overlooking the bay, it was built in 1837. It was designed by an architect called Sandham Symes, who happened to be a nephew of local developer Robert Warren. The latter commissioned the former to design many big houses around Killiney Hill.

Inside Mount Eagle, there's still a magnificent wooden model of the house made to the orders of its architect, and it shows the striking Y shape of the house. The model also carries the signature of Sandham Symes.

Like its near neighbour, Ayesha Castle, Mount Eagle was built with local granite, but the design of the two houses is totally different. Mount Eagle was designed in the neo-classical style, while inside, the plasterwork is done in the Greek Revival style. The amount of detail in the house is reflected in the design of the adjacent stables, which have cut stone details. The house is also noted for its very fine and broad terrace, which gives magnificent sea views.

MOUNT SALUS, OFF KNOCKNACREE ROAD, DALKEY

Mount Salus in fact comprises two early Victorian houses, a pair of semi-detached houses built in 1841, period architecture at its best, with the porticos and bay windows. They are at the end of a private cul-de-sac.

Number 1 Mount Salus features four bedrooms, three bathrooms and a wine cellar. When it went up for sale in 2005, the price tag was €4 million. When No. 2 Mount Salus was put up for sale in 2019, the price tag was lower, €2,850,000, but its history is more interesting. While the house has full facilities, including a reception room, a dining room, a living room and a kitchen on the ground floor, and on the return, a library, a conservatory, and a family room, on the first floor, it has five bedrooms, one more than No. 1 Mount Salus.

In 1854, when Cardinal Newman was in the middle of establishing a Catholic university in Dublin, which is now University College, Dublin, he lived at No. 2 Mount Salus, then occupied by his sister. The Cardinal wrote that the place was as beautiful as it was healthy. He noted that the Wicklow Mountains could be seen from one window, while from the other window could be seen Kingstown (now Dún Laoghaire) and Howth Head. The Cardinal commented: 'I never saw a place out of Italy and Sicily like it for the beauty of rock and sea'. In 2019, the cardinal was made a saint.

NIAGARA VILLA, DALKEY

This stunning Victorian house with four en-suite bedrooms, a south-westerly facing private walled garden and lovely sea views from its location on the Coliemore Road, was up for sale in the summer of 2019. The price tag was €2.5 million.

PALERMO, KILLINEY

This enormous and lavish house, built in 1848 on the Killiney Hill Road, was the work of the Hone family, related to the famous Irish artist, Nathaniel Hone. The house also has a separate mews, built in the original stable yard. The house was given an Italian name, like many other houses and roads in the area.

In the early 1970s, Louis O'Sullivan and his wife Fionnuala bought the house, at a time when few people wanted to move to Killiney. By 2017, they had decided to sell up, so that they could move to Sutton, on the other side of Dublin, to be close to their son Patrick, who is now running the family business of antiques, art and craft fairs. In 2017, the asking price for Palermo was €4 million, but a year later, it had dropped by €1 million.

Palermo has another claim to fame. Bono's home is just below it on the hill running down to the coastline at Killiney.

ROCKVIEW, DALKEY

Rockview, a Victorian house on the Coliemore Road in Dalkey, has an unusual design to its front face and from its rear, spectacular views over Dublin Bay. It was on the market in early 2019 for €5 25 million.

ROSENEATH, DALKEY

Few employers leave a substantial house to one of their employees, but that is exactly what William Morris, a local man of great wealth, did. After he died in 1861, the property on Coliemore Road came into the possession of his housekeeper, Elizabeth Armstrong. A decade later, she had the house demolished and Roseneath built on the site, a fine building that still stands today, just a two-minute walk from Coliemore Harbour.

SAINTBURY HOUSE, KILLINEY

This early nineteenth-century house was one of the few houses built in Killiney before the arrival of the railway. Maureen O'Sullivan, born in 1911, lived in what was then her family home until she was 18, when she left for America to begin her long career as a Hollywood film star. She died in the US in 1998, aged 87.

The house was bought in 2019 for nearly €2.3 million by Kevin Nowlan, chief executive of Hiberian Reit, a large Dublin property company renowned for its substantial profits. The house had been on the property market since 2016 and took two and a half years to sell. Its initial selling price was €2.95 million.

SAN ELMO, VICO ROAD, DALKEY

This vast mansion was built in 1870 for a man called Henry Hayes, a wealthy tanner. The house was built on high ground overlooking Killiney Bay and Hayes also had built a square viewing tower in the extensive grounds. Hayes had it built for use by his daughter and it was said that the highest room in the tower had a grand piano. However, many years later, in 1986, the tower was struck by lightning and as repairs were impossible, it was demolished.

SORRENTO TERRACE, DALKEY

The views from the rear of the eight houses at Sorrento Terrace, across Killiney Bay to Bray Head and the Wicklow mountains, are the best from any private houses in Co. Dublin, unparalleled in their majesty. As for the terrace of houses, it was one of the most ambitious building projects in the Dalkey area, although a much larger earlier plan was for twenty-two houses. A similar project had been proposed in 1840 by Robert Warren of Killiney Castle, who wanted to build a development on Killiney Hill called Queenstown. But it came to nothing.

The land for the houses at Sorrento Terrace was owned by a barrister called Hercules Henry Graves MacDonnell and he leased out the land for building. He stipulated that at least £1,000 had to be spent on each house and that the proportions, appearance and uniformity of the terrace had to be maintained at all costs. The houses were built by Edward Masterson, from Kingstown, now Dún Laoghaire, who had a high reputation for quality.

Sorrento Terrace, Dalkey, and behind it, Dalkey Island.

The end house on the terrace was slightly larger than the rest of the houses and its grounds took in all the lands at Sorrento Point. The first owner of this end house was MacDonnell himself.

In the 1890s and early 1900s, when the end house, Sorrento House, was owned by a judge called Thomas Overend, regattas were held on the immediate coastline by the Dalkey Amusements Committee. Guests during the regattas were entertained on the lawns of Sorrento House. It was also planned that there should be a promenade, open to all, by the shore below Sorrento Terrace, but this was never developed.

STRAWBERRY HILL, VICO ROAD, DALKEY

This was one of the first houses to have been built in the Vico Road. It's a single-storey house, over basement, designed in the Italian style and complete with a short tower. It was built in 1850 and its first owner was a man called Stevenson, who was the general manager of the gas company in Dublin.

In the late 1960s, Strawberry Hill became the subject of considerable local controversy. The then owners of the house wanted to demolish it and build an eighty-bedroom hotel in its place. In 1967, planning permission was refused, although the then minister for local government overturned this decision and gave approval for the scheme. But fortunately, the scheme never came to anything and the planned hotel was never built.

A decade later, in 1861, a pair of houses was completed on the Vico Road for Henry Gonne; these are the houses that stand below the Vico Road and directly above the railway line at the Vico bathing place. The features of these houses included large bay windows, which gave exemplary views over Killiney Bay, but they also included storm shutters, essential for winters in this exposed location.

STRATHMORE, KILLINEY

The former Canadian ambassador's residence, this house, dating from the 1860s, was sold in 2015 to a US entrepreneur, Dr Joe Elias, who paid €7.5 million. Initially, he had intended to demolish it, but instead, he retained most of the existing structure and got planning permission for a massive extension of over 1,700m².

When the Canadian government bought the house back in 1957, they paid C$54,000 for it.

SUMMERHILL, MARINO AVENUE WEST, KILLINEY

One of the most expensive houses ever sold in the area, Summerhill was put on the market in 2019 for the small sum of €10 million. This magnificent detached Victorian residence was built around 1850 to provide around 700m² of accommodation. Upstairs, it has five substantial bedrooms and a total of five bathrooms. The accommodation stretches over three floors and on a lower level, the principal reception rooms all face south to the sea. One of its star attractions is the kitchen, which is large enough to have a substantial sitting and dining area, with windows giving great views out over Dalkey Island. There's a coach house beside the main house, suitable in earlier days for staff accommodation, although these days, residents in the area are usually much less likely to have live-in staff.

Outside, the 2 hectares of grounds include a long, sweeping driveway, floodlit tennis courts, a golf putting and chipping green, as well as manicured lawns, and a feature waterfall and pond. From the house itself and its gardens, there are spectacular views over Killiney Bay, Sorrento Terrace and Dalkey Island.

THE GROVE, KILLINEY

This house, built around 1840 on the slopes of Killiney Hill, close to what is now Bono's house, started life as a hunting lodge. In more recent times, second and third floors were added and even a home theatre, before it was converted into a nursing home. The house was put up for sale in 2019 for €4.5 million, despite needing extensive renovation.

TUDOR HOUSE, DALKEY

This vast house, just off Castle Street in Dalkey, was put up for sale in 2019 for €3.5 million. It was built in 1845 for a wealthy surgeon, Richard Parkinson, using stone from Wolverton Castle, once one of the seven medieval castles that guarded Dalkey. The house was designed with six bedrooms and its floor space of 600m² is six times the size of an average Dublin home. The grounds are comparatively small, about 0.3 hectares, but in recent years, the gardens were designed by star garden designer, Diarmaid Gavin.

TUDOR LODGE, KILLINEY

Tudor Lodge at Violet Hill, off Church Road in Killiney, was put up for sale in 2015 with a price tag of €2,950,000. It's a six bedroomed house with a total area of 597m². When it had been put up for sale previously, in 2004, the house was a sixth smaller than it is today and it went on the market for €2.25 million.

Although the Church Road area is an attractive part of Killiney, houses there rarely fetch prices similar to those in nearby Killiney Hill Road.

Arch over Victoria Road, near its junction with Killiney Hill Road.

VICTORIA HOUSE, COLIEMORE ROAD, DALKEY

This extraordinary residence, complete with a huge turret, stands on 0.8 hectares on the Coliemore Road, Dalkey. It was built in the early 1860s by James Milo Burke, who also built the nearby big houses of Sorrento and Springfield.

The house was built complete with adjoining stables and a coach house, as well as with extensive gardens, while the house itself had no fewer than sixteen rooms. In 1916, the house suffered extensive fire damage, which cost £10,000 to repair, a cost fortunately covered by insurance. The house, which at the time was owned by the then president of the Dublin Chamber of Commerce, Richard Booth, had to be completely rebuilt. Only the original and very striking turret remained.

Today, the house has three reception rooms on the ground floor, four bedrooms on the first floor, and three more bedrooms on the second floor.

In 1943, Victoria House was bought by Senator John E. McEllin. After he died in 1969, his wife, Una, sold the house and gate lodge in 1976 to the McEllins' daughter, Dara Lenehan, and her husband. The Lenehans, well-known for the Lenehan's hardware business in Dublin, kept the house until 2001.

Bids were expected of over €6 million, but none came. The house stood empty for three years, until 2004, when businessman Gerry Kelly bought it for €5.5 million. But it seems that the main reason Victoria House hadn't sold was because its development potential had been completely exhausted by previous owners. Buyers were much more interested in houses that still had lots of development potential.

Altogether, a total of ten additional houses have been built in recent years in the grounds of Victoria House; they include the Dalkey Sound housing development. But the sea views from Victoria House are protected by restrictive covenants that the heights of the houses built around its boundary on Coliemore Road are restricted, so that whoever is living in Victoria House continues to enjoy unrivalled views across Dalkey Sound to Dalkey Island. The best sea views from Victoria House are from the studio that's inside the turret; they are said to be absolutely amazing.

THE YELLOW HOUSE, KILLINEY

Built in 1890 and containing an original eighteenth-century Gesso fireplace, this house is about 400m from Killiney DART station. In 1993, Ned O'Hanlon, a video producer, and his wife, Ann Louise Kelly, bought the house. They sold it on in 2017 for €1.9 million.

9

PUBS, RESTAURANTS AND HOTELS

BENITO'S, CASTLE STREET, DALKEY

This restaurant and pizzeria has been trading for about fifteen years and specialises in home-made pasta, wood-fired pizza, grilled meats and seafood. It also offers a takeaway service.

CAFÉ DE LA GARE, KILLINEY

The café in the DART station at Killiney comes with many recommendations; reviews on TripAdvisor say that this is the best tea and coffee place in Killiney.

DEMOLISHING THE OBJECTIONS TO CAFFÉ NERO IN DALKEY

In 2014, Caffé Nero, which claimed to be the largest independent coffee retailer, had just opened its first café in Dublin and wanted to open up in Dalkey, at Number 26 Castle Street, Dalkey. But the opening was vigorously opposed by locals, who threatened to boycott it if it did open. Many locals said if it did ever open, it would spoil the uniqueness of Dalkey, which at that stage had twenty locally owned cafés.

In July 2014, writer Eamon Delaney, in the *Irish Independent*, demolished the objections to Caffé Nero starting up in Dalkey, which it never did. He said that when he was a young nipper, living in Dún Laoghaire, he and his confréres were always known as the 'Railway Children', because many of them who lived in the south Dublin coastal belt travelled by train as far as Lansdowne Road to attend Marian College on Lansdowne Road. There was always a big contingent of children from Dalkey. Delaney said that the children were always a real social mixture, very much at odds with the current view of privileged southside brats with Dort accents and designer clothes. In fact, he said, they reflected Dalkey's mixed legacy as an old fishing village with working-class cottages and the humble homes of people who worked in the port of Dún Laoghaire.

However, he noted that in recent years, the small seaside village of Dalkey, along with adjacent Killiney, had been transformed into 'Dalkey sur mer', a highly sought after oasis for for celebrities and media people. He said that these famous residents included Bono, Neil Jordan and racing driver Eddie Irvine, while the local pub, Finnegans, which had just been visited at that stage by Michelle Obama, wife of the former US President, who was on an official visit to Ireland, could seem like the VIP room of RTÉ on certain nights. Delaney also said that with a lobster festival and a book festival, the whole place had become very heritage and hanging basket. He added that the new Dalkeyites would do well to remember the town's roots, as controversial comments had been made by some local residents as they tried to prevent the opening of the chain coffee shop in the town. Concerned residents, many of them other coffee shop owners (surprise, surprise), felt that the opening of Caffé Nero would lower the tone and commercialise the intimate but upscale town. According to an online petition, 'the proposed development of a non-sympathetic disproportional protected structure would aggressively distort the nature of other local family businesses in our heritage town and distract from sustainable development, unbalancing local commercial business.

It could contribute to the takeover of the local main street by corporate chains, while independent, community-based outlets go under.'

Eamon Delaney said that this was a ridiculous assertion, representing social engineering and protectionism at its worst. It was also anti-free market and anti- competition and deprived customers of variety and choice. Delaney also pointed out that Caffé Nero is a highly reputable outfit, the biggest independent coffee retailer in Europe, with more than 650 stores in seven countries. He also said that the company had plans, in 2014, to invest a further €20 million in Ireland over the next five years, creating up to 350 jobs in forty outlets.

Commented Delaney: 'the Dalkey elitists should bear this in mind as they try to prevent the opening of new businesses. And it's not as if Dalkey, however well-heeled some of its inhabitants, doesn't need the business'. He pointed out that one of the reasons why David McWilliams created the Dalkey Book Festival was because he was moved by the sharp decline in retail trade in the town. 'Dalkey may be like some rustic Long Island bolthole for some, but for others, it is another struggling Irish town, with chip shops and empty retail spaces'.

Far from ruining its image, a Caffé Nero could add to the town's prestige and add to the cash-rich footfall of locals and tourists alike, he concluded.

CASTLE CHINESE RESTAURANT, CASTLE STREET, DALKEY

This restaurant is noted for its huge menu of what it describes as authentic Chinese cuisine. Around thirty years ago, Castle Street was noted for another Chinese restaurant, the Kingsland, a branch of a Dublin city centre restaurant.

CORNER NOTE CAFÉ, COLIEMORE ROAD, DALKEY

This café opened in 2011 with the aim of serving great food at incredible prices. It is open six days a week, but is closed on Mondays. Its new evening seafood restaurant, Bait, is open from Thursdays to Saturdays.

DALKEY ISLAND HOTEL

One of Dalkey's vanished hotels, Dalkey Island Hotel was in a Regency villa dating back to the 1830s. The hotel was noted for its wooden Liberty furniture and its quiet and comfortable atmosphere. But in 1997, plans were approved to demolish the hotel and build a luxury apartment complex on the site. When the development was completed, the apartments were sold for around IR£1 million each, making them the most expensive apartments in Ireland at the time.

Two other old hotels, also on the Dalkey coastline, suffered the same fate as the Dalkey Island Hotel. The Shangri-La Hotel and the Khyber Pass Hotel both gave way to apartment developments; in the case of the Shangri-La, the Pilot View apartments were built on the site.

DE VILLE'S RESTAURANT, CASTLE STREET, DALKEY

This traditional bistro-style restaurant was opened in 2012 by brother and sister David and Kim O'Driscoll, serving modestly priced traditional bistro fare, accompanied by wines, mainly French, craft beers, an extensive range of spirits and house cocktails.

The Druid's Chair pub, Killiney.

DRUID'S CHAIR PUB, KILLINEY

A traditional, classic style pub, the Druid's Chair is located near the brow of Killiney Hill, on a site that offers spectacular views over Killiney Bay, as far as Bray Head.

FINNEGAN'S BAR, SORRENTO ROAD, DALKEY

This pub, which dates back well over 100 years, was once known as O'Meara's. The big change came when Dan Finnegan bought the premises in 1970. He had returned to Dublin in the mid-1960s after a decade in Canada and he and his brother Peter took over a small pub in Bride Street, near Christ Church Cathedral. Then came what he described as a gamble, when he bought the pub in Dalkey from Joe Larkin. It has continued in the ownership of the Finnegan family ever since and Dan Finnegan's sons, Alan, Donal and Paul, all became involved in its management.

Finnegan's pub, Dalkey village.

Major refurbishments were carried out in 2001 and 2005 but the original Victorian façade and many of its interior features were retained.

Over the years in the ownership of the Finnegans, the pub has attracted many of the stars who live in the area, such as Bono. The late Maeve Binchy and her husband, Gordon Snell, often came here, as their house was just across the road.

FITZPATRICK'S CASTLE HOTEL, KILLINEY

The main building dates back to the 1740s and has been extensively renovated since then. In 1840, the name was changed from Mount Malpas to Killiney Castle by the then owner, Robert Warren. During the 1939–1945 Emergency, the private house was requisitioned by the government and used as army billets. It didn't become a hotel until 1971, when the late Paddy Fitzpatrick, a Dublin hotelier, and his wife Eithne, a former model, took it over. Paddy Fitzpatrick died in 2002, but the hotel is still in the Fitzpatrick family, run by Paddy and Eithne's daughter, Eithne Fitzpatrick Scott-Lennon.

Paddy had grown up on the Vico Road in Dalkey, so he knew the area well. His first wife, Eithne, died in 1993 and four years before his death, he married his second wife, Nora. Before he died, Paddy Fitzpatrick bought five more hotels, in Ireland and the US, including two in Manhattan, New York. Just a year before his death, he spent $27 million on a hotel in Chicago.

Today, the Fitzpatricks' hotel in Killiney is a four-star establishment, situated in lovely gardens, with spectacular views out over Dublin Bay. It has 113 en suite rooms and thirty-six family rooms. Facilities include an indoor swimming pool and gym, while regular weekly entertainment is organised, in addition to entertainment at Christmas and the New Year. The hotel has three dining options: PJ's restaurant, the Mapas restaurant and the Library Bar.

FUEL FOOD, RAILWAY ROAD, DALKEY

Fuel Food opened in 2015 as a wholefood kitchen and deli, a whole new approach to eating out, developed by Oliver McCabe. The premises had started, in 1959, as the Select Stores, a general grocery shop run by his parents, Paddy and Margaret McCabe.

THE GUINEA PIG RESTAURANT, RAILWAY ROAD, DALKEY

Arguably the most famous restaurant in Dalkey, it started in 1957 and was run from 1978 by the Stewart family. Renowned for its seafood, it has often attracted stars filming at Ardmore Studios in Bray, the likes of John Ford, Peter Ustinov and John Wayne, as well as Meryl Streep, Liam Neeson and Cliff Richards. Many celebrities living in the area have also dined there over the years, including the late Maeve Binchy, the late Hugh Leonard, Bono, The Edge, Enya and Lisa Stanfield.

When Mervyn Stewart was running the restaurant, he was the subject of many jibes from Hugh Leonard in his weekly column in the *Sunday Independent*, all of which helped propel the restaurant to even more fame. The restaurant was put up for sale in 2017 and was bought by Jérome Fernandez, a French restaurateur who also owns La Réserve in Ranelagh. He pledged to continue with the timeless decor and the fine dining in Dalkey.

JAIPUR, CASTLE STREET, DALKEY

This elegant restaurant, designed in a contemporary style, is renowned for its cutting-edge Indian cuisine. It seats seventy, is open daily and is also vegetarian friendly.

KILLINEY COURT HOTEL

This hotel, near the Killiney DART station and Killiney beach, closed down in 2006 and was demolished, replaced by apartments. The original house at the heart of the hotel was one of a number of big houses built in Ireland between 1863 and 1865 that were inspired by designs of French chateaux. But from the 1970s onwards, a series of extensions of mediocre design created what one planning consultant said was a hotchpotch of pastiche Parisian, Rhineland follies and dismal Dublinesque.

However, the hotel was widely used by local residents. Despite the campaign to save the hotel, its demolition and the subsequent construction of blandly designed apartments went ahead.

KILLINEY SHOPPING CENTRE

This shopping centre has a number of restaurants and eating places, including Pizza Hut, Masala Indian restaurant and the Green Dragon Well, a Chinese restaurant.

KING'S INN PUB, CASTLE STREET, DALKEY

A traditional style pub on Castle Street, it is also noted for its regular weekly performances of traditional and bluegrass music.

KINGSLAND CHINESE RESTAURANT, CASTLE STREET, DALKEY

Around thirty years ago, the Kingsland Chinese restaurant at 24 Castle Street, a branch of a city centre concern, was popular. It succeeded the China Garden at the same address, which was above The Picture House video rental shop on the ground floor.

LEE'S KITCHEN, RAILWAY ROAD, DALKEY

This Chinese takeaway is a popular spot with Dalkey residents and visitors to the area. Around forty years ago, next door to where Lee's is now, close to the corner of Railway Road and Castle Street, Chez Lahiffe restaurant was popular, although now it is long gone, like most of the old-time cafés and restaurants in Dalkey.

MAGPIE INN, COLIEMORE ROAD, DALKEY

This cosy, traditional pub, part of the Dalkey drinking scene for well over fifty years, became insolvent in 2014 and secured the protection of the High Court. Its insolvency was blamed on cashflow issues and a dispute with the landlord of the premises. In 2012 and 2013, the pub had been turning over more than €1 million a year.

But fortunately, this stylish pub, renowned for its food and drink, has managed to keep going since that blip in its trading

The Magpie Inn, Dalkey village.

fortunes. At the time of writing, it is still going strong, with generally favourable reviews for its food and drink on TripAdvisor.

1909 RESTAURANT, CASTLE STREET, DALKEY

The 1909 restaurant is a traditional type of restaurant, with façade to match, at 31 Castle Street.

THE QUEEN'S BAR, CASTLE STREET, DALKEY

The oldest pub in Dalkey, opposite the Catholic church on Castle Street, it dates back to 1745. It was originally called The Queen's Royal Hotel. Over the years, many renovations have been carried out and today its facilities include the Steak Room restaurant and the Vico, an Italian restaurant.

The Queen's Hotel, Castle Street, Dalkey.

RESTAURANT NOVA, COLIEMORE ROAD, DALKEY

This restaurant opened in 2017, specialising in world cuisine; American, Asian, Italian and Mexican influences are seen on its menus.

RISTORANTE RAGAZZI, COLIEMORE ROAD, DALKEY

This small but lively Italian restaurant has theatrically inclined waiters, according to a well-known critic, Georgina Campbell. It serves dinners from Tuesdays to Sundays.

ROLLAND'S RESTAURANT, KILLINEY

This was once one of the premier restaurants in the area, started by Pierre Rolland in 1975. He had been the head chef in the renowned Russell Hotel on St Stephen's Green in Dublin, which closed down in 1974. The restaurant in Killiney was run by Pierre's son, Henri, and it lasted for twelve years before closing down in 1986.

STARBUCKS

The international chain of coffee shops had a short-lived existence in Dalkey, where many residents were very opposed to its starting up in the town in 2008. Such was the strength of the local boycott that the Dalkey Starbucks closed down in November 2009, after little more than a year's trading.

THAI HOUSE, RAILWAY ROAD, DALKEY

This restaurant and takeaway opened in 1997, making it one of the longest surviving businesses of its kind in Dalkey.

THE CLUB, COLIEMORE ROAD, DALKEY

The second oldest pub in Dalkey opened in 1847 as the Queenstown Tavern. It also served as a morgue, a dual-purpose use that lasted in the Irish pub trade until 1962.

At one stage, this pub was owned briefly by a priest. When Anne Williams, the then owner, died in 1928, she left the pub to a local priest, Revd Fr Canon John Kelly, the parish priest of Sandyford. He kept it for eleven months, then sold it on to Edward Murphy in 1929, for the grand sum of £350.

In 1944, the pub's name was changed to The Club, but it failed to realise its potential. It was sold again, in 1969, and the new owner, Seamus Sheeran, carried out many renovations that have helped carry the pub through to the present day.

10

REMARKABLE PEOPLE

MAEVE BINCHY

Maeve Binchy, one of Ireland's most popular writers during the past fifty years, had close connections with Dalkey for most of her life.

She was born in Dalkey in 1939 and brought up there. Her initial career was as a teacher at a girls' school on Pembroke Road, Ballsbridge. If a class proved too rowdy, she simply went across the road to Searson's pub until the pupils had quietened down. But her real forte was writing and she joined *The Irish Times* as a journalist. At one stage, she was the London editor of the newspaper.

Her first book came out in 1970, a collection of her newspaper articles, while her debut novel was *Light a Penny Candle*, which came out in 1982. Altogether, she wrote sixteen novels, four short story collections, a play and a novella. Her books were immensely popular, boosted by her endearing personality.

But well before she had published her first novel, she had met and married Gordon Snell. Maeve Binchy had gone to the BBC in London to record a piece for *Woman's Hour* on Radio 4 and while she was at the BBC, she met Snell, a freelance producer for the corporation. They married in 1977 and for a while afterwards, they lived in London, before settling down in Ireland. For many years, the couple lived close to the centre of Dalkey.

Maeve Binchy died in July 2012, and her death prompted an amazing outpouring of grief and sorrow from her innumerable fans. Since her death, her husband has continued to live in the same house in Dalkey, where he says 'her presence is very much still here'. He has continued his own career as an author of children's books.

MARTIN BIRRANE

Martin Birrane was a property investor who had a strong interest in motor racing; he bought Mondello Park in Co. Kildare in 1986. Many of his property interests were based in London, but this Co. Mayo native bought a massive mansion in Killiney in the 1980s, Kenah House in St George's Avenue, off Killiney Hill Road. This house was set on 1.2 hectares; it was built in 1871 and had an enormous tally of rooms, thirty-two in all. Martin eventually sold the house, in 2005, for a quarter of the €8 million he had originally sought. It was bought by Brian Long, co-founder and CEO of Parthus Technologies. Martin Birrane, the tailor's son from near Ballina, died in June 2018, aged 82.

BONO

Bono and U2 have been among the superstars of Irish rock for the best part of forty years and are household names around the world. But Bono, U2's frontman, and band member The Edge and their families, have lived in Killiney for many years. Bono's first residential link with Killiney came when he and his family moved to Killiney Hill in the early 1980s, a far cry from his early days, when as a youngster, he was brought up in Finglas, on Dublin's northside, where he had his primary education at the local national school. He did his secondary education at Mount Temple comprehensive in Clontarf, before beginning his first moves to form a band. U2 was founded in 1976.

His wife is Alison Hewson and they have two daughters and two sons. Besides his incredibly long-lasting musical career, Bono is also a noted philanthropist.

Bono is on record as saying that Killiney is a great place to live, with wonderful neighbours. He has also said, 'you can really unwind here and as an added bonus, you never get hassled in the street'. But the homes of Bono, at Temple Hill on the Vico Road, and The Edge at Sorrento Cottage, on the divide between Dalkey and Killiney, are strictly off limits to prying eyes.

The Edge, otherwise David Howell Evans, was born in Essex in 1961, and is married to Morleigh Steinberg, a Californian-born choreographer and dancer.

Other entertainers with close links to the area include the popular BBC and ITV presenter Gloria Hunniford, who was born and brought up in Portadown. She and her husband bought an apartment at the Bartra development in Dalkey in 1998. Another Northern-born entertainer, Van Morrison, also has a property in Dalkey, Kilross House on Sorrento Road.

CHRIS DE BURGH

Chris de Burgh, the singer, born in 1948 and best known for his 1986 song, 'The Lady in Red', has long had connections with Dalkey. At the height of his career, in the 1980s, he and his wife, Diane, lived in Dalkey, and it was there that he had his infamous affair with their au pair, Moresa Mason, although it didn't emerge into the public domain until 1994. Then Chris de Burgh and his family moved to a sprawling estate in Co. Wicklow, before renewing their connection with Dalkey. They put their Co. Wicklow house and estate up for sale in 2019.

CYRIL CUSACK

Cyril Cusack, who was born in 1910 and who died in 1993, was one of the best known, well-regarded actors of his generation, and had long time connections with Dalkey. He had three daughters and two sons.

Niamh Cusack, who also became an actor, was born in Dalkey on 20 October 1959 and was raised in Dalkey. Sinéad Cusack, who also became an actor, had been born there on 18 February 1948. In 1967, she gave birth to a boy and gave him up for adoption; he is Richard Boyd Barrett, a TD and a noted left-wing politician. The following year, 1968, she married actor Jeremy Irons.

One of Cyril Cusack's two sons, Pádraig, was born in Dublin on 16 March 1962; he is a theatre and TV producer. His other son, Paul, has long worked in RTÉ Television.

JOHN DOWLAND

John Dowland was a remarkable composer of poetry, songs and instrumental music during the first Elizabethan era. He lived from 1563 until 1626. He was a close friend of William Shakespeare. His melancholy music is still performed today. A well-known Irish historian, W.H. Grattan Flood (1857–1928) claimed that Dowland had been born in Dalkey, although no proof of this has ever come to light. However, there's some evidence that Dowland did have close connections with Dublin in his early life.

ENYA

Enya, the noted singer-songwriter, lives in an extraordinary castellated mansion in Killiney called Manderley Castle, which dates back to 1840. She was born Eithne Pádraigin Ní Bhraonáin, in Gweedore, Co. Donegal, in 1961, and started her singing career with her family's group, Clannad, in 1980, going solo two years later. By 2001, she had sold forty-six million albums worldwide and was worth close to €40 million. She had bought the castle in Killiney in 1997.

In 2005, the *Sunday Times* rich list revealed that the reclusive singer was worth €100 million; as recently as 2016, she was said by the same newspaper to have been worth €91 million. One of her most recent albums was *Dark Sky Island*, released in 2016.

Apart from being, at one time, the biggest selling singer in the world, and immensely wealthy, Enya has been troubled on occasions by stalkers. On one occasion, in 2005, a stalker broke into the castle and tied up a maid. He spent two hours searching unsuccessfully for Enya, who had hidden in a panic room. After she had bought the castle, she had the walls surrounding it heightened, then had the walls topped off with 1m-high railings.

HUGH FARRINGTON

Hugh Farrington is a man with extensive property interests in Dalkey, where in 2011, the *Irish Mail on Sunday* revealed that he and his wife, Sheryl, could choose between several multi-million-euro properties that they own. Their properties there have included Elsinore on Coliemore Road, an apartment in the Bailey View complex, an apartment at Berwick House on Coliemore Road and a luxury house at Rockfort Avenue.

In 2011, the *Irish Mail on Sunday* revealed that Hugh Farrington was famed for selling some of the most expensive petrol in Europe, while he had also been convicted of using faulty pumps that delivered too little fuel at the Usher's Quay service station in Dublin.

THEODORA FITZGIBBON

A noted cookery writer and food critic, Theodora FitzGibbon and her film-maker husband, George Morrison, lived at

Coliemore Road, Dalkey, in a grace and favour arrangement with the owner of the house. Subsequently, the house they lived in was bought by Vincent Browne, one of the most controversial personalities in Irish media, in print journalism as well as in radio and television, as a home for himself and his family.

Theodora FitzGibbon was born in London in 1916 and much of her early work was done in Paris, in the late 1930s, where she worked as a nude model. In 1944, she married an Irish-American writer, Constantine FitzGibbon. The marriage lasted fifteen years, but she kept his surname. In 1960, she married again, to George Morrison, who has had a long career as a film director.

Theodora wrote many books on cookery and for many years she was the chief food critic of *The Irish Times*. She was noted for her outrageous sense of humour. A couple of years before her death, she sold a Henry Moore sculpture she owned, which enabled her and Morrison to buy their own house, not far away from where they had lived for so long. She died in Killiney in 1991.

PADDY FITZPATRICK

Paddy Fitzpatrick, a well-known hotelier in Killiney, died in 2002. Born in Dublin in 1930, his father, John, managed two pubs in Dublin: one in the Coombe, the other in Pimlico. After the pubs were sold, the money was invested in Guinness shares – so much so that Paddy Fitzpatrick often joked that the family was reared on Guinness dividends. He went into the hotel business and eventually became the manager of the Doyle Hotel Group. After a falling out, Paddy decided to set up his own hotel business, beginning in 1970 with what became the Fitzpatrick Castle Hotel in Killiney. He expanded the business in Ireland, including to Bunratty, as well as in the US. His wife, Eithne, a former model, was a key figure in the hotel business, but she died in 1993.

After the death of his mother, son John set up the Eithne Fitzpatrick Memorial Fund, which became the Eithne and

Paddy Fitzpatrick Memorial Fund in 2002. The hotels in the group are still going strong, including the one in Killiney, a four-star establishment that's now owned and run by Eithne and Paddy's daughter, Eithne Fitzpatrick Scott-Lennon.

WILLIAM HOGG

William Hogg, a noted industrial archaeologist, has lived in Dalkey for many years. Between 1997 and 2012, he compiled a comprehensive history of milling in Ireland and he is also the life president of the Mills and Millers of Ireland association, which he founded in 2001.

In 2015, he was given a lifetime achievement award by the Industrial Heritage Association of Ireland.

JOHN DE COURCY IRELAND

A great maritime historian, Dr John de Courcy Ireland lived for many years at a modest house on Dalkey Avenue. Born in India in 1911, the son of a Co. Kildare man who was serving in the British Army, he went to Marlborough College in England. When he was 17, he ran away and took on a job as a deckhand on a Dutch freighter sailing to South America. When he returned, he went up to Oxford, where he met Beatrice (Betty) Haigh; they were married when they were both 21.

At home in Ireland subsequently, he had a long career as a teacher, including at Newpark Comprehensive School in Blackrock, Co. Dublin. But his strong interest in maritime matters lasted his whole adult life. He was a founder of the Maritime Institute Ireland in 1943, was a co-founder of the National Maritime Museum of Ireland in Dún Laoghaire in 1959, and was secretary of the Dún Laoghaire lifeboat for over twenty-five years. He also wrote many books about the sea and his last book, in 2001, was about the history of Dún Laoghaire Harbour. He and his wife Betty were committed to many left-wing causes. She died in 1999 and he in 2006.

Seat in Castle Street, Dalkey, in memory of Harry Latham.

HARRY LATHAM

Harry Latham, born in 1922, had an encyclopaedic knowledge of Dalkey's history and often conducted guided historical tours through the town. His book, *Walks in Dalkey*, was published in 1983, while in 1993, he contributed to a book on St Patrick's Church of Ireland in Dalkey.

Just after he died, Dalkey Community Council held its twenty-ninth AGM in Our Lady's Hall and as a mark of respect to a great friend of the council, a minute's silence was observed. Five years later, a commemorative stone seat was unveiled in Dalkey in his memory.

HUGH LEONARD

Hugh Leonard, noted playwright, TV dramatist and *Sunday Independent* columnist, had close connections with Dalkey for most of his life, having been raised there by his adoptive parents after being born into very poor circumstances. His birth name was Jack Keyes Byrne.

Born in 1926, he began his career as a civil servant, working in the Land Commission, where he started to use his nom de plume, Hugh Leonard, to hide his literary work from his civil servant bosses. His first known performance came in 1944, when he worked as an extra on the film *Henry V*, largely shot on the Powerscourt estate in Co. Wicklow and starring Laurence Olivier.

His civil service career lasted for fourteen years; the first play he had produced was *The Big Birthday*, performed at the Abbey. He went on to carve out a spectacular career for himself writing TV and film scripts in Britain; he earned so much money that he was able to buy a Rolls-Royce car and a boat on the River Shannon. When he died, in 2009, he left an estate worth €1.5 million. This was despite Russell Murphy, a well-known and at the time, respected accountant, who swindled vast amounts of money out of Hugh Leonard and other well-known figures such as Gay Byrne. Hugh Leonard was very upset by the fact that Murphy used his (Leonard's) money to pay for expensive seats for his other clients at some of the theatrical performances of Leonard's plays.

Apart from all his work for the theatre, films and television, Leonard also wrote a long-standing and spectacularly acerbic column for the *Sunday Independent*.

Hugh Leonard's first wife was Paule, a Belgian woman, who died in 2000. Subsequently, he married Katherine Hayes. For many years, Hugh Leonard lived in an apartment at Pilot View, Dalkey, where the other inhabitants were six Siamese cats.

NEIL JORDAN

Neil Jordan, born in Co. Sligo in 1950, has a formidable reputation as a film director, a screenwriter and a novelist. From his first film in 1982 right up to his most recent, he has directed just over twenty films, for most of which he wrote the screenplays as well.

He lives at Sorrento Terrace in Dalkey and like many other well-known residents in the Dalkey and Killiney area, he hasn't avoided property disputes with neighbours.

Jordan has five children, two from his first marriage, to Vivienne Shields, a solicitor, while he also has two from his current marriage to Brenda Rawn, his personal assistant.

He also has one from a relationship he had between 1998 and 2001 with Mary Donohoe, an architect.

PAT KENNY

Pat Kenny, one of Ireland's best known radio and TV presenters, is a long time resident in Dalkey. He was born in Dublin in 1948; his father worked in Dublin Zoo. Pat Kenny began his forty-one-year career in RTÉ as a continuity announcer. He presented *The Late Late Show* from 1999 to 2009, when he handed over to Ryan Tubridy. Pat then went on to present other TV shows, such as *Prime Time*, while he had a long-running show on Radio 1.

He left RTÉ in 2013 and since then has continued as a programme presenter with *Newstalk*, while he also does TV work.

Pat and his wife Kathy bought a site in Dalkey in 1988, built their home there and have lived there ever since. However, they had long and costly legal battles over proposed developments on the adjacent Gorse Hill site, as they sought to retain their family's privacy. At the end of 2018, they won their battle. Their one-time neighbour and long-time adversary was Gerard Charlton, a retired solicitor. He died in 2015 and left an estate valued at €3.1 million.

HOWARD KILROY

Howard Kilroy was a well-known businessman who lived for many years in Dalkey. He died in May 2019, at the age of 83.

In business, he was best known for his role at Smurfit Kappa, having joined the Smurfit Group in 1973 as financial controller. He was also a director of the Bank of Ireland and of Cement Roadstone Holdings. In 2009, he sold his Smurfit shares, which brought his net worth to €42 million.

Apart from his business interests, Kilroy had a keen interest in Scouting at world level and chaired the investment committee of the World Scout Organisation, while he also chaired the Irish arm of the Baden-Powell fellowship.

He is survived by his wife Meriel and five children, as well as seventeen grandchildren and four great-grandchildren.

ALLI MACDONNELL

Alli MacDonnell was a successful model and mother of four, who tragically died in February 2019.

She had close connections with Dalkey and her funeral was at the Church of the Assumption. She was buried at Roscrea, Co. Tipperary.

Alli had a successful twelve-year career in modelling and went on to become a regular contributor to Virgin Media One's Ireland AM TV show. One of her children, Harry, was diagnosed with autism in 2016 and she went on to campaign for Ireland Autism Action. She is survived by her four children, Alex, Sara, Harry and Siena Rose. Sadly, her former boyfriend, Andrew Mann, a singer, died in May 2019.

DAVID MCWILLIAMS

David McWilliams, economist and media commentator, has long lived in Dalkey, where he and his wife, Sian Smyth, a former corporate lawyer who comes from near Belfast, founded the Dalkey Book Festival held every June. They also have a summer home in Croatia.

McWilliams, who was born in 1966, trained as an economist and has since built up a substantial reputation as an economics adviser and lecturer, as well as being a frequent media columnist on the subject, arguably the best-known economics commentator in Ireland. He has also made TV documentaries and has hosted many radio and TV shows.

VAL MULKERNS

Val Mulkerns was a distinguished writer who lived in Dalkey for many years; she died in March 2018, at the age of 93. Val's father was an actor and she was brought up in Fairview, on Dublin's northside. Her family's precarious finances meant that they couldn't send her to university; instead, she got a temporary job in the civil service. As soon as she was made permanent, however, she left and went to England, where she worked as a teacher for three years, despite the fact that she didn't have any relevant qualifications.

In 1953 she married Maurice Kennedy, a civil servant and writer, and put her career on hold while she brought up her three children. Initially, she and Maurice lived in Rathgar before moving to Sorrento Road in Dalkey. She was a great swimmer and walker, noted for climbing Killiney Hill.

Mulkerns' first novel had come out in 1951, and after she resumed her career, her output became prolific, including as a contributor to the RTÉ Radio 1 Sunday Miscellany programme. She also wrote extensively for the old *Evening Press* newspaper in Dublin and was a member of Aosdána.

She was noted for being a feminist before her time, and campaigned extensively for LGBTQ rights and for marriage equality.

LENNOX ROBINSON

Lennox Robinson was a noted playwright and theatrical producer, a leading figure in the later stages of the Irish literary renaissance and long associated with the Abbey

Theatre. He was born in Douglas, Cork city, in 1886 and died in Dublin in 1958. For much of his adult life, he lived at Sorrento Cottage in Dalkey.

TOM ROSS

One of the most colourful sporting characters ever to grace the sporting scene in Dalkey was Tom Ross, a leading figure in the local swimming club for many years. He was instrumental in building the long-standing changing rooms on Bulloch pier. When the Australian swimming team was in London for the Olympics in 1948, he persuaded them to come over to Dublin for a two-day gala at the old baths in Blackrock under the banner of the Dalkey Swimming Club. The gala was a great success, with a full crowd. Later on, in the 1960s, Tom Ross was chairman of Dalkey United Football Club.

GEORGE BERNARD SHAW

George Bernard Shaw, the dramatist and philosopher, spent most of his life in England but had a close connection with Dalkey in his younger days. Shaw was born in 1856 at Synge Street at Portobello, Dublin, and was brought up there. When he was 10, he and his family moved to Torca Cottage at the end of Torca Road in Dalkey, close to the Cat's Ladder at the end of the Vico Road, until 1874.

He spent much of the rest of his life in England, where he died in 1950.

Shaw had a spectacularly successful literary career, working into his early 90s. He was the only writer ever to win both a Nobel Prize for Literature and an Oscar.

As for Torca Cottage, it had been built on the site of a quarryman's cabin. In Shaw's time, the cottage was quite small, but the views from it were tremendous. In 1947, the Dalkey Development and Protection Association put up a plaque on the cottage, in honour of Shaw.

In more recent times, the cottage was much extended and now has five bedrooms. In 2016, the then owners put it on the market for €2.45 million.

JIM SHERIDAN

Jim Sheridan, born in Dublin in 1949, has had a spectacular career in the film industry, as a director, producer and screenwriter. He was born and brought up in Dublin's north inner city. Between 1989 and 1993, two of the films he directed, *My Left Foot* and *In the Name of the Father*, received thirteen Academy Award nominations.

He had a close connection with Dalkey, having paid IR£1.2 million in 1998 for a fisherman's cottage on the Coliemore Road. Over the following decade, he spent €5 million on the property, completely redesigning the house, by then known as Martha's Vineyard, which sits right on the edge of the water. But there were building problems and a long legal case. In 2015, the property was sold for €2.3 million, a far cry from its former price tag of €10 million. In 1992, Sheridan bought a house in St Mary's Road, Ballsbridge, as the family home, selling it on in 2019.

JOHN SIMPSON

John Simpson, born in England in 1944, spent his whole career with the BBC, which he joined in 1966. His first posting to Ireland came in 1972. In covering world affairs for the BBC, he visited 140 countries and interviewed 200 heads of state. He says his greatest moment was seeing the joyful arrival in power in South Africa of Nelson Mandela in 1994.

Simpson has been married twice; his second wife being Dee Kruger, a South African. They lived in Dalkey, near Bulloch Harbour, for a number of years before returning to live in the UK in 2005. However, he has returned to spoken at the Dalkey Book Festival on various occasions in the years since.

GORDON SNELL

In April 2019, the *Irish Independent* carried a detailed interview with Gordon Snell, the husband of the late Maeve Binchy. They had lived together in Dalkey for many years. She died on 30 July 2012.

In the interview, Gordon Snell's eyes appeared to be twinkling as he said 'please excuse the mess' as he waved a hand over the clutter of books and photographs he had gathered together for the purpose of the interview. Although it is now over seven years since she died and Gordon is now aged 87, she is still everywhere in the house, from lots of photographs to copies of her many books, including the sixteen novels she wrote. 'Her presence is very much still here', Gordon told the interviewer, Orla Neligan. He said that there are still many members of Maeve Binchy's family living nearby, great friends who look out for him. He also has two cats, Audrey and Fred, who are great company.

He revealed how they met when he was working as a freelance radio producer with the BBC in London, when Maeve arrived to do an interview for *Woman's Hour* on Radio 4. They clicked immediately, then got married shortly afterwards, in 1977. The pair were married for thirty-five years and even though they were both writers, in Gordon's case, of children's books, they always worked well together and were each other's fans. They neither relished nor disliked their global celebrity.

The writer of the piece said that there was a childlike and endearing quality to Gordon Snell, despite his 87 years. His parting advice to the writer was 'take notice of your daydreams'.

11

SCHOOLS AND COLLEGES

CASTLE PARK SCHOOL, DALKEY

A prestigious privately-run junior school, Castle Park is co-educational and caters for children from 3 to 12. It also has Montessori facilities and a wide range of extra-curricular activities. The school has a long history, going back over 110 years. The headmaster is Denis McSweeney.

DALKEY SCHOOL PROJECT

This school opened its doors in 1978 as a three-teacher school, with ninety-two pupils, in a Victorian house in Vesey Place, Dalkey. The parents involved wanted an inclusive school that embraced tolerance and encouraged mutual respect. Today, there's a flourishing network of eighty-four primary school and thirteen second level ones. Educate Together schools are attended by 28,000 pupils.

Forty years on, the Dalkey School, whose principal is Miriam Hurley, staged a special event to commemorate the founding of the school.

GLENAGEARY KILLINEY NATIONAL SCHOOL, KILLINEY

The school is co-educational under Church of Ireland management and it is linked to St Paul's church in Glenageary, Holy Trinity church in Killiney and St Matthias church, also in Killiney. The school has 250 children, from junior infants to sixth form, studying a wide range of subjects. The school has one teacher for every class.

The school principal is Sadie Honner, while the deputy principal is Elaine Wolfe.

HAROLD BOYS' NATIONAL SCHOOL, DALKEY

This school is under the patronage of the Catholic Archbishop of Dublin and of Dalkey's parish church.

The enrolment at the school is about 120 and its principal is Teresa Buckley.

In 2002, a major refurbishment of the school included the construction of an extension and a redevelopment of its play areas and grounds.

The school has a wide range of sporting activities, including GAA and rugby as well as basketball and swimming. Extra-curricular activities include chess, computing and drama.

HOLY CHILD SCHOOL, KILLINEY

This highly regarded girls' school was founded in 1947, in the old County Hotel in Killiney. It began with thirty-four pupils, under the aegis of the Society of the Holy Child Jesus, an order of Catholic nuns.

The school grew rapidly, both in student numbers and in reputation, and the first big expansion came in 1950, when a new wing was added, which included more classrooms, a library and a school hall. More development came in

1962, when a new school hall was built, complete with its innovative wall of stained glass.

Its first lay principal was Vera Collins, appointed in 1996. She was followed by Geraldine Hackett in 2007, while the current principal, Caroline O'Brien, took up the position in 2019. The school is a member of the Le Cheile Trust.

LORETO ABBEY, DALKEY

This privately owned, fee-paying school has a long history. It is a member house of the Institute of the Blessed Virgin Mary, whose history, around the world, goes back to the seventeenth century. The Irish branch of the Institute was founded in 1821 by Frances Ball, a native of Dublin. Her first foundation was at Rathfarnham and was called Loreto Abbey; the Sisters became known as the Loreto Sisters and all subsequent foundations, at home and abroad, took the same name.

Loreto Abbey was founded in Dalkey in 1843. While Frances Ball was negotiating the purchase of the site, on the seashore, which she bought in 1842, she rented Bulloch Castle, where she ran a boarding and day school, from 1841 until 1843. She designed the new school in Dalkey herself and it was built with Dalkey granite. The new boarding and day school opened on 17 August 1843. The boarding school lasted until 1982.

Today, the day school has about 630 day pupils and seventy members of staff. The principal is Robert Dunne.

Among notable past pupils of Loreto Abbey is Hilary Frayne Weston, 26th Lieutenant Governor of Ontario in Canada. Her husband, Galen Weston, is a businessman whose interests include the Brown Thomas department store in Grafton Street, Dublin.

ST JOSEPH OF CLUNY SECONDARY SCHOOL, KILLINEY

This is a privately run secondary school for girls, located in Killiney and founded in 1956. It has a broad curriculum and a wide range of sporting activities. The principal is Mary White, while the deputy principal is Orla Lambert. Like the Holy Child School, it is a member of the Le Cheile Trust.

ST PATRICK'S NATIONAL SCHOOL, HARBOUR ROAD, DALKEY

A co-educational Church of Ireland school, it caters for children aged from 4 to 12, from junior infants to sixth class. About 100 children attend the school, whose principal is Philip Salter. The whole school attends assembly in St Patrick's church, Dalkey, on a weekly basis. The rector of the church is the chair of the board of management. The school states that funding from the Department of Education and Science isn't enough to cover expenditure, so voluntary contributions are always welcomed. The school building was constructed in 1870 at a cost of over £1,000, paid for by a parishioner, Charles Leslie. The school was designed by Edward H. Carson, a Dublin architect. He and his wife, Isabella Lambert, had six children. Their third son was also called Edward Carson. He was a barrister, famously defending the Marquess of Queensbury against the libel case brought by Oscar Wilde, and Unionist politician, who was eventually knighted, becoming Sir Carson. He later became a Lord. Carson was largely responsible for the creation of the Northern Ireland state, founded after the Government of Ireland Act in 1920, which brought the Stormont parliament in Belfast into being.

12

SHOPS OLD AND NEW

CLEGG'S

This shop, in Castle Street, which does key cutting and shoe repairs, is a real veteran of the retail trade in Dalkey, there since the early 1930s.

COUNTRY BAKE

Specialising in a wide range of delicious home baking, Country Bake also serves breakfast and lunch in its upstairs dining room. The shop has been in Castle Street for over twenty-five years.

Country Bake home bakery, Castle Street, Dalkey.

DAISIE STONE

This arts and craft shop on Railway Road, Dalkey, is a quirky giftshop, considered among the best shops of its kind in the Dublin area. All the items it sells are Irish-made.

DALKEY ARTS

This art gallery at 19 Railway Road shows the work of a wide range of artists, everything from traditional to abstract, while it also offers over fifteen years of experience in framing.

DALKEY NEWS

A long-established newsagents, in addition to newspapers and magazines, it sells a wide range of items such as stationery and greeting cards. It also has a special area devoted to toys and gifts for children, and the staff are renowned for never rushing kids into deciding what they want.

DALKEY PHARMACY

This pharmacy, at Railway Road, which is noted for its striking brick and stone façade, is a beautiful old traditional pharmacy that was established in 1877, making it the oldest shop in Dalkey. However, two pubs, The Club and The Queen's Bar, are older. The Dalkey Pharmacy is owned and run by Blaithin O'Brien.

FINANCIAL INSTITUTIONS

Financial institutions in the area include AIB, at Castle Street, Dalkey, and the EBS building society, also in Castle Street. The EBS also has an outlet in the Killiney Shopping Centre. Dalkey Credit Union's offices are in Castle Street. The area also has two post offices, one at Ulverton Place, Dalkey, the other in the Killiney Shopping Centre.

FIRE ABOVE DALKEY SHOP

The block containing the New to You shop in the centre of Dalkey caught fire five years ago. Despite the fire brigade arriving within seven minutes, the whole building was quickly destroyed, but the elderly woman who lived in the upstairs flat, Grainne Neligan, was rescued and taken to hospital. After the fire, friends, neighbours and local firms rallied around to raise money for the rebuilding of Grainne Neligan's home and the shop below it.

FRED'S TRAVEL AGENCY, CASTLE STREET, DALKEY

Many travel agents' shops have succumbed to online bookings, in keeping with world-wide trends. In Dalkey, Fred's Travel at 3A Castle Street, which was very popular for around thirty years, has long since gone.

GOLDEN APPLE

For anyone wanting a good selection of vegetables, this shop at 21 Castle Street is a welcoming retail outlet.

GRAPEVINE WINE SHOP

The Grapevine wine shop was set up in 1999 to sell wine as well as import, and has a wine bar and an art gallery. Patrons can enjoy both food and wine on the premises. The gallery, for art exhibitions, is above the wine shop and was opened by Siobhan Bastable in 2016.

HANDWORKS

Located at 39 Castle Street, this shop specialises in a wide range of individual gifts as well as a great selection of cards.

HICKS

Hicks butcher's shop in Castle Street is one of Dalkey's long-established retail establishments and it's particularly noted for its sausages.

KERIN'S PHARMACY

Based in the old tramway office in Castle Street, this pharmacy has been trading since 1985. It was put up for sale in late 2016, with an asking price of over €1 million.

KILLINEY SHOPPING CENTRE

The Killiney Shopping Centre, built about forty years ago on Rochestown Avenue, has a wide range of retail outlets, including Euro Spar and SuperValu supermarkets. SuperValu also has a supermarket at Castle Street, Dalkey, which used to be a branch of the old Quinnsworth.

In the Killiney centre, other outlets include Paddy Power, the bookies, and a branch of Peter Mark, the chain of ladies' hairdressers. Ladies' fashion, hardware and travel also feature, while restaurant outlets include Pizza Hut, an Indian and a Chinese restaurant.

KILLINEY STORES CLOSES

The old Killiney Stores, at the corner of Strathmore Road and Killiney Hill Road, closed in May 2018. The shop had been

The old Killiney Stores, Killiney.

run by the Clarke family since 1963, when they took over what had been the Bayview Stores, run by the Rush family.

While Dalkey has a network of streets at its centre that have many retail outlets, Killiney doesn't have anything similar. However, when the Rush family was trading in Killiney, the village then had another shop that also doubled as the post office.

LADIES' HAIRDRESSERS IN DALKEY

Local hairdressers include Rhona's hair salon at 20 Castle Street, Rosemarie's hair salon at 23 Castle Street and The Head hair salon, at St Patrick's Road.

MAXWELL'S PHARMACY

Maxwell's is a renowned pharmacy at 28 Castle Street, Dalkey, next door to Dalkey News. It occupies an imposing single-storey building that is topped with a distinctive

Maxwell's Pharmacy, Castle Street, Dalkey.

balustrade. The owner is Greg O'Lublai, who is also the superintendent pharmacist. The pharmacy was established in 1879 and it has always traded from the same location on Castle Street.

MOLLS

Molls, at Railway Road in Dalkey, has a wonderful cover-all-angles description of its merchandise: paraphernalia. Also in Railway Road is a more precisely defined retailer, James Murphy, a jeweller.

ON THE GRAPEVINE

This wine shop at 21 St Patrick's Road has a good selection of French and other wines and for a small corkage, patrons can buy a bottle of wine and consume it on the premises. There's plenty of seating in the shop as well as upstairs and customers can enjoy such food as tapas with their wine.

O'BRIEN'S OFF-LICENCE

This shop, in Castle Street, part of a large chain, lost a long-standing employee, Carl O'Brien, who was a legend in the district. He died in June 2019. One customer, Maeve Kennedy, said that she never saw him in a bad mood and that he always had a smile and a joke for every customer, even if, like her, they spent half an hour choosing from the cheapest bottles of wine!

PAPERMINT

This popular shop in Castle Street sells all kinds of paper goods, including stationery and wedding gifts.

SELECT STORES, DALKEY

The Select Stores traded in Dalkey for over sixty years, having been founded in 1959. Over the years, various shops were started on the site, including a greengrocers and a wine shop, and it now houses Fuel Food. Before the Select Stores opened at the corner of Railway Road and Castle Street, Ma Reilly's was a popular newsagent in the same location.

THE GUTTER BOOKSHOP

The Gutter Bookshop at 20 Railway Road is a high point for book lovers in the area. The original shop had opened in Temple Bar, Dublin, in 2009 and the shop in Dalkey opened four years later, in 2013. The aim of the bookshop has always been to provide something different from chain bookstores. In 2017, the bookshop was named the independent bookshop of the year for Ireland and Britain.

Apart from many book-related events, such as storytelling for children, this shop also specialises in gifts, with children's puppets being very popular. It also runs three book clubs and provides books for local festivals, such as the Dalkey Book Festival. It also has a strong relationship with bestselling Dublin crime writer, John Connolly.

The owner of the bookshop is Bob Johnston, who has been in the book trade for thirty years and knows it inside out. But what he most loves doing is talking to people about books. Although the shop is small, it stocks plenty of new titles and also has a substantial backlist, while it also has an ordering service for hard-to-find and out of print titles.

PHOTOGENIC PHOTOGRAPHY

Specialising in family portraits, the firm was founded in 1991 by Barry and Margaret Moore, both of whom have photographic qualifications. Barry worked as a photographer with what is now Eir, but left to form the company with Margaret. Among the team are Sacha O'Kelly and Kieron Meagher.

Another photographic outlet is the Dalkey Photo Centre in Castle Street.

SHOPS AND TRADERS OF DALKEY PAST

In Dalkey in 1960, a wide range of retailers and other traders existed, most of whom are long since gone.

In Castle Street, they included O'Toole's grocers, one of six on the street; Totterdell's boot and shoe repairs; Bannons the fishmongers; the dispensary, which provided home assistance for poorer families; Findlater's the grocers and wine merchants, Searsons wine and spirit shop; a branch of the Dartry Dye Works and a branch of the Limerick Creamery.

Railway Road shops included Bradys, confectioners; McGloines, butchers; Hayes, Conyngham & Robinson, the chemists; Miss Sullivan, tobacconist; Holmes the grocer, and the Castle View café.

On nearby Coliemore Road, there was the Ritz guesthouse while at Coliemore Villas, Arthur Lawson, a journalist, lived and worked, described as a correspondent to trade journals.

Many of Dalkey's old shops, up to a century ago, were recalled in detail in *Dalkey: An Anthology* (Mullen, 2008). One woman remembered that when she was a young mother in Dalkey, she could leave her pram and baby outside McLoughlin's shop at the corner of Coliemore Road and either head off to Dún Laoghaire or have a little time to herself in Dalkey, while the shop staff in McLoughlin's looked after her pram and baby. Very often, there was more than one pram left outside the shop. Changing times indeed!

The 'mother and baby' and 'father and son' shop at the corner of Castle Street and St Patrick's Road was also remembered as a great place to shop, with such a wide range of stock, including hand-smocked children's dresses, that there was no need to go to either Dún Laoghaire or Dublin city to shop.

The chemist's shops in old Dalkey were as good as any doctor's surgeries. Maxwells, Hayes, Conyingham and Robinson and Fillers were all excellent; Maxwell's is still trading in Castle Street today. If children were unwell or had a minor accident, the staff and owners in the various chemist's shops were always ready with successful cures and never a mention of health warnings or possible side effects.

In the old days, Findlater's was the main grocery shop in Castle Street, selling a wide range of groceries, including fresh food, and a good selection of wines and spirts. The cash office overlooked the whole shop; in those far off days, there were no cash registers and the sales assistants had to load the sales dockets and the cash into small tubes that were carried by overhead wire to the cash office. If change was given, it came back the same way. At the time, Findlater's seemed a large shop and it was always fascinating to see babies in their prams watching the containers of cash crossing the wires that ran overhead the length and breadth of the shop.

For many years, Gemma's newsagents, which is long since closed, was the only newsagents and stationers on

Castle Street, run by the Heneghan family. Mr Heneghan, the shop owner, was helped in the shop by his son Peter, a very quiet and kind young man who tragically lost his life in a traffic accident on 20 September 1966. On the Sunday morning following the accident, Gemma's was closed. The town went into a state of shock as the news of the accident spread. What was once the long-standing premises of this family-owned-and-run shop is now the Ulster Bank.

There were lots of other small shops in Dalkey in those far-off days, nearly all of them long gone. Mary Newport had a small grocery shop beside what was then the post office, run by Dave Langan. She sold groceries, as well as Wexford-grown vegetables, but eventually she married and the family moved to Wexford. The old post office was converted into Don Giovanni's restaurant. Mr White had a shoe repair shop that stood across the street for Joe Dowd's shop, which sold sweets, minerals and ice cream. His shop was taken over in due course by Noel and Kathleen Byrne, who opened a fruit and vegetable shop there.

The Golden Gift shop, beside the old tram yard, was a great place to shop for presents to suit every occasion. Castle Street also had a couple of butcher's shops in the old days, Dunnes and Grimes. Subsequently, Doyles became the only butcher's shop left on Castle Street. Mick Byrne had a lovely fish shop at the end of the town, near McDonagh's. Queues would form outside it on a Friday morning, at a time when it was customary for people to abstain from meat on that day and settle for fish instead.

On Tubbermore Road, Paddy McCabe ran another vegetable shop. He is remembered as a kind and gentle person, who built up a great business. He always wore a beige-coloured shop coat and at Christmas time, he'd pull numerous pieces of paper from the pockets with customers' names and what they had ordered for Christmas. Tragically, he died at a young age, leaving his wife and five children, but his wife continued to run the shop with great success.

Out of this litany of old shops in Dalkey, only a couple survive today, including Maxwell's pharmacy and Clegg's, the key cutting and shoe repair shop on Castle Street that has been there since the 1930s. In the old days, Willie Clegg was a genius at hand-stitching repairs to shoes.

These days, the retail scene in Dalkey has changed completely, but Castle Street still has the air of a village street, characterised by locally owned and managed shops and an absence of big international retail chains.

STATION HOUSE

This basement gallery, at Sorrento Drive, close to Dalkey DART station, opened in June 2017. It's an independent gallery devoted to showing and promoting contemporary photographic work by Irish and international artists. Dalkey's newest art gallery is Southshore Arts, also near the DART station.

TRAMYARD BOOKSHOP

The old tramyard in Dalkey used to have the €3 bookshop, in which children's and general books sold for €3 each, or four for €10, very similar to booksellers in old Dandelion market in Dublin. In 2018, a review of this bookshop on TripAdvisor hoped that it would reopen, but this seems unlikely now that the tramyard has been sold for redevelopment.

A number of other businesses are based in the tramyard, including Aran Candy, The Big Foot driving school and Dee's nail salon, and it remains to be seen what will happen to them in the light of the planned development.

XTRAVISION

Over a decade ago, a now defunct retail chain, Xtravision, which sold and rented videos, was based at 24 Castle Street. The premises now houses Roberts, a fresh food retailer.

13

SPORT

CUALA GAA CLUB, DALKEY

This leading GAA club is based in a sports and social centre in Dalkey, while it also has playing facilities in nearby areas such as Shankill. Its grounds in Dalkey were redeveloped in 1989. The club has a winning track record going back many years, including winning the All Ireland senior club hurling championships in 2017 and 2018, as well as wins in camogie and ladies' and men's Gaelic football.

In Dalkey, there's a long history of Gaelic games, going back over a century.

The Cuala Hurling Club was founded in 1918, while the St Mary's Camogie Club came into being in 1948, changing its name in 1982 to the Cuala Hurling and Football Club. Today, it's the Cuala Hurling, Football and Camogie Club. The St Begnet's GAA club was founded in 1957, while a decade later, the Cuala Boys and Roger Casement Club for minors was established, later becoming the Cuala Casements.

DALKEY ROWING CLUB

This club promotes traditional skiff racing in Dalkey. Its first regatta of the season is usually the one organised by St Michael's Rowing Club in Dún Laoghaire. Recently, the Dalkey club got a new east coast skiff, which was hand-built by a local craftsman, Terence Keogh. It was funded by the sports capital programme and locally raised money.

DALKEY SCOUTS

The 17th Dalkey Scout Group has been in existence in Dalkey since 1927. Its group leader is Martin Ellard and the scout den is at the top of St Begnet's Villas. One of the group's previous long-term leaders was Donnchadh O'Shea, who died in 2007. The Dalkey Scouts have five age groups, with the youngest being the Beavers, for boys aged between 6 and 9, while the oldest are the Rovers for 18- to 21-year-olds.

The Irish Girl Guides are also active in Dalkey. In 2019, Joan Gregg received a fifty-year service award for her long contribution to Irish Girl Guides. From 1962 until 1971, she was captain of the Girl Guides in Dalkey and one of the local organisations with which she is still involved is the St Patrick's dramatic society in Dalkey.

There's also a Sea Scout troop in Dalkey, with the same age categories as the Dalkey Scouts. The Sea Scouts are a more recent formation; having started at a meeting in St Patrick's school hall in1956, they now have around 120 members.

DALKEY SCUBA DIVING CLUB

This recreational scuba diving club was founded in 1976 by Shane and Ollier Gray, who now run diving and hill walking holidays at El Hierro in the Canary Islands.

Until the late 1980s, the club was run from a house on the Coliemore Road in Dalkey called Roxborough. Then it moved to Dún Laoghaire, where it has been based ever since, at the marina. The club has about forty members and to date has trained over 1,000. During the summer, club members dive on Wednesday evenings and on Sunday mornings, while in winter, there's a snorkelling meet on Sunday mornings at

Coliemore Harbour. The club also makes frequent trips to the west of Ireland. To raise funds for the RNLI, it organises a snorkel around Dalkey. The club also has a lively social side, with barbecues, parties and other events, not forgetting its always memorable Christmas party.

DALKEY SWIMMING CLUB

The Dalkey swimming club was founded in 1937 by three local men, Thomas Hamilton Ross, who became the president, James J. Byrne, who became the handicapper, and Jimmy McGlone, the starter. On the pier at Bulloch Harbour, the club built a rectangular structure so that members could enter the water safely. During certain tides, such as spring tides, Bulloch Harbour can drain of water completely. The swimming club lasted until 1999, when it was wound up.

DALKEY UNITED

The local football club promotes the sport in the area for all age groups and its facilities include high performance skills. It uses mostly Hyde Park in Hyde Road Dalkey for its matches, but some take place at Hudson Road and at Shanganagh Cliffs, in Shankill.

Among its teams are three girls' teams; in 2019, the under II girls advanced to the Irish Rail cup final, while the under 10 girls had an undefeated season in 2019. The club also has adult men's and women's teams.

FITZPATRICK CASTLE HOTEL, KILLINEY

The hotel has a wide range of sporting facilities, including a fully equipped gym and a 20m indoor swimming pool with an ondeck whirlpool spa and Scandinavian wood saunas. A very popular swim programme is organised for children

Fitzpatrick's Castle Hotel, Killiney.

of all ages. The hotel also has Olympic lifting areas and a fitness studio.

KILLINEY GOLF CLUB

This renowned local golf club opened in 1903 and its full nine-hole course was opened for play on Easter Monday that year. The decision to form the club had been made at a meeting in Killiney town hall on 5 June 1902. Three local men, all described as members of the local gentry, played key roles in setting up the club; they were Captain E.P. Stewart, George C. Ashlin and George F. Stewart. Within a month, the club, which is based at Ballinclea Road, Killiney, had 300 members. A centenary book about the club was published in 2003.

The club has had thirty-three presidents, up to and including the 2019 president, Michael Thunder. The 2019 men's captain is Brendan Barrett, while the 2019 women's captain is is Miriam McCullough.

Apart from its excellent golfing facilities, the club is also noted for the food served in its dining room. The head chef is Mark Clarke, who formerly worked at the Westbury Hotel in Dublin, while the maître d' is Gerry White.

LORETO ABBEY SPORTS HALL

The impressive new sports hall at Loreto Abbey is available for use both by pupils at the school and the local community. The hall can be used for a wide variety of indoor sports, while outside, a full-size hockey pitch can be sub-divided into small-sided football matches.

Outside, a multi-purpose hard surface can be used for such sports as basketball and tennis.

SEAPOINT RUGBY CLUB

This rugby club, based at Churchview Road in Killiney, plays adult and youth rugby. Its teams include a 1st XV, a 2nd XV, a 3rd XV and an under 20 team. In youth rugby, it has the Seapoint Dragons, while it also plays mini rugby. Included in the highlights of the year, the club has its AGM towards the end of April, while the annual dinner is held the same day.

SNOOKER

Dick Brennan from Dalkey was one of the best amateur snooker and billiards players to represent Ireland. These sports were very popular in Dalkey in the early twentieth century, although that's not the case these days. The old snooker and billiard club operated at the back of Ma Reilly's newspaper shop, at the corner of Castle Street and Railway Road, and it often featured in Hugh Leonard's stories about life in Dalkey in the old days.

While snooker had faded away in Dalkey before the Second World War, it got fresh impetus when Joe Baker's saloon was set up over Hick's butcher's shop on Castle Street in 1950. The saloon became a great social centre and many epic tournaments as well as several exhibition games were staged there. Local people who were very much to the fore in these games included Gerry Mooney, Michael Hayde, George Ellard, Pat and Peter Heneghan, Joe Sharkey, Paddy McDonald and Eddie Hick, all as chronicled in the pages of *Dalkey: An Anthology.*

14

TRANSPORT

DALKEY ATMOSPHERIC RAILWAY

The Dalkey Atmospheric Railway, which was vacuum-operated, ran for nearly ten years, from August 1844 until April 1854.

It was built by the great railway pioneer William Dargan on the trackbed of an earlier tramway, which had been built in 1817 to carry stone from Dalkey Quarry to the harbour that was then being built at Kingstown.

The atmospheric railway had a steep incline and the track had a gauge of 1,435mm, which is the standard gauge for the modern railway system in Ireland. Power for the train came from the 380mm vacuum tube, which ran alongside the rail lines. The vacuum came from a pump house at the top of the line. However, the vacuum tube fell just over 500m short of the station at Dalkey, so the trains relied on their own momentum for the last part of the journey. To start the journey in the opposite direction, trains had to be pushed by hand until they connected with the vacuum tube.

On the ascent from Kingstown to Dalkey, the train was able to get up to speeds of 64kph, using the motive power of the vacuum tube. Descending the line, under gravity, the trains went even faster. Trains ran every half hour between 8 a.m. and 6 p.m. and could carry over 200 passengers at a time. This very novel means of train propulsion attracted a lot of attention from newspapers around the world, putting Dalkey in the spotlight, but a planned extension to Bray never happened.

After the railway closed in 1854, part of the line was integrated into what is now the mainline and DART line. The bridge that carried the railway over Castle Park Road still exists. The pumping station was in the grounds of a house that still stands at The Metals, close to Barnhill Road. The name is also preserved in that of Atmospheric Road, close to Barnhill Lawn.

DALKEY'S 'GHOST' STATION

Long ago, Dalkey had another railway station, Obelisk Hill, situated between the present-day stations at Dalkey and Killiney. It opened in June 1855 and closed at the beginning of January 1855, shortly before the first Killiney station came into operation.

DALKEY RAILWAY STATION

This station opened on 10 July 1854 and was the successor, on a different site, to the Dalkey station on the old atmospheric railway. What is now the present Dalkey station was closed to goods traffic in 1964 and subsequently closed to all traffic. It was reopened in 1983, prior to the arrival of the DART electric train service, which started the following year, going as far as Bray and eventually extended to Greystones. The tunnel just south of Dalkey station is 160m long.

DALKEY TRAIN CRASH, 1979

The Dalkey train crash, which happened on 16 November 1979, was serious in that forty-one of the people on board the two trains had to be taken to hospital, but it could have been much worse.

Two trains travelling in opposite directions collided in an area known as the Khyber Pass, difficult to access because of the steep inclines on both sides of the track. About 100 people, mostly schoolchildren, were on the trains. Tommy Doyle, one of the drivers, was the most seriously injured; it took rescue workers three hours to free him from the wreckage of his cab.

Another railway incident happened in Dalkey on 18 July 2018, when a train was a attacked by someone throwing stones. Fortunately, the train wasn't damaged, nor were any passengers injured.

DALKEY TRAMS

Dalkey was the terminus of the last tram route to run in Dublin, the Number 8, which started its journey at Nelson's Pillar.

It had started with the Dublin Southern Districts Tramways company, which, in 1879, opened the extension to the line from Nelson's Pillar, bringing the trams as far as Dalkey. The line between Kingstown and Dalkey was 1.2m gauge, with passing loops. The track was subsequently upgraded to standard Irish gauge.

In 1896, the tramway companies in Dublin were merged into one entity, the Dublin United Tramways Company, controlled by William Martin Murphy. That same year, the entire line to Dalkey, which had used horse-drawn trams, was converted to electric propulsion.

The last tramline in Dublin closed down on 9 July 1949, and huge crowds turned out in Dalkey to see the last tram. The crowds became so uncontrollable that Radio Éireann's plans to record the last tram in Dalkey had to be abandoned. Souvenir hunters also helped themselves to anything that wasn't nailed down.

Dalkey's old tram depot, just off Castle Street, was built in 1879, and most of the old tram sheds survive today, although underused. Sections of the old tram tracks leading to the depot can still be seen. In 2018, the 0.2-hectare site was sold to a developer for €3 million, but as of the summer of 2019, building work to transform the site had yet to begin.

After the Dalkey tram was closed down, the Number 8 route number passed to buses and the Number 8 bus route survived until 2015. At that stage, Dublin Bus said that improvements to the Number 59 bus route had rendered the Number 8 route surplus to requirements.

The old Dalkey tram sheds.

KILLINEY STATION

The original Killiney railway station opened in 1858 and lasted until 1882, when it was replaced by a new station, named Killiney and Ballybrack. The latter had had a station from 1854 until 1882. From 1882 onwards, Killiney station remained open, unlike the station in Dalkey, and it too became a station on the DART line in 1984.

15

WORK

DALKEY CREDIT UNION

On 9 May 2019, the Dalkey Credit Union celebrated its golden jubilee in considerable style. It had grown out of the Dalkey Savings Group, founded in 1966, and was one of the first credit unions to open in Ireland. One of the key figures in the early development of the credit union movement in Ireland was Nora Herlihy, who lived at Tubbermore Road, Dalkey, for a number of years.

When the Dalkey Credit Union opened, a key figure was Michael Kennedy, who became the first honorary secretary. The first registered office was at Number 8, Dalkey Park, which was his home. Within a very short time of the credit union opening, it had 110 members, with a total of £750 in savings. For many years, it has had its offices in Castle Street, Dalkey, and is part of a wider network that has six other branches in south Co. Dublin.

DALKEY OFFICE PODS

At 20–21 St Patrick's Road, Dalkey, office pods are available for rent. These are high-spec offices suitable for one, two or three people. The location also has stylish meeting rooms.

GUINNESS BARGE NAMED *KILLINEY*

In 1927, the Guinness brewery in Dublin started taking delivery of ten barges, to take barrels of stout down the River Liffey to ships waiting to go to Britain. All the barges were given Irish place names, with one being called *Killiney*. The fleet was withdrawn from service on Midsummer's Day 1961.

OIL BONANZA THAT NEVER HAPPENED

In 2012, there was much speculation that drilling for oil could begin off the coast of Dalkey and on the Kish Bank, 10km out to sea, with many people believing that Dalkey could be transformed into a Dallas-style oil town. It was said that there was a 20 per cent chance of oil being found. But it all came to nothing. In 2019, Tony O'Reilly, the chief executive of Providence Resources in Donnybrook, Dublin, said that due to delays with foreshore legislation, the company did not drill the Kish Bank in 2013 and that there have been no subsequent operations in the area.

WORK OPPORTUNITIES IN DALKEY AND KILLINEY

Most such opportunities are in the hospitality sector, especially with restaurants in Dalkey. There used to be half a dozen hotels in Dalkey, but none exist today, and Killiney has just one. Pubs in the area provide some work opportunities, otherwise the main ones are in retail, again in Dalkey, but also in the Killiney Shopping Centre. There is some work for nursing and general care staff in the limited number of nursing homes in the area, while diplomatic residences can offer jobs as housekeepers and similar staff. Babysitters and childminders are also in demand across the area. Some professional sectors such as architecture and design also offer some work opportunities.

ZAHRA MEDIA GROUP

This group, which says it is one of the leading cross-platform media groups in Ireland, was founded in Dalkey in 2003 and remained there for many years. As recently as 2012, it was based in Railway Road, Dalkey, although it's now in Bray.

Among its print publications are *Easy Food* and *Easy Parenting*, while it also makes extensive use of digital technology.

KEN THE FERRYMAN

The man with the best job in Dalkey is undoubtedly Ken the Ferryman, who takes people across Dalkey Sound, from the tiny Coliemore Harbour to a small inlet on Dalkey Island. He is always known simply as Ken the Ferryman and few people know his second name, something he never reveals, even on his Facebook page. But his maritime knowledge of the area is second to none; he has been an oarsman with rowing clubs in the Dalkey area for the past forty-five years and comes from a family steeped in the maritime history and practicalities of the Dalkey area.

His boat is the *Lilly Rose*, named after his granddaughter who sadly died soon after she was born. The boat was commissioned as a passenger ferry, even though it carries just half a dozen passengers, but she is ideally suited for negotiating Coliemore Harbour as well as the small inlet on Dalkey Island used for passenger landings. Like all such boats in Irish waters, it has to be stringently tested each year by the Department of the Marine. Ken himself holds all the marine qualifications needed for his job. The boat also carries a complement of life jackets suitable for all ages.

Ken starts his service to Dalkey Island each April and it runs until the beginning of October. The boat runs every day of the week, from 10 a.m. until 6 p.m., although after-hours crossings can be made by appointment. The fares are reasonable, €10 for an adult and €5 for under 18s.

If the weather is fine for the crossing, it's absolutely idyllic for the passengers and wonderful too for the captain, Ken the Ferryman, who continues to love the job he has been doing for so long.

BULLOCH HARBOUR

The history of Bulloch Harbour, as recalled in *Dalkey: An Anthology*, shows that it has been used by local fishermen for centuries.

In the 1930s and 1940s, one of those fishermen was Paddy Smyth, who was the quartermaster on the mail boat, the Leinster, which was sunk off the Kish Bank in October, 1918, shortly before the First World War ended. He had switched shifts, so he wasn't aboard the Leinster the night she sank. Until quite recently, many other local fishermen worked out of Bulloch Harbour to earn a living. Going back close on a century, fishermen would often employ a helper, who would get a third of the catch, while the fisherman himself took two-thirds of what was landed. In the 1930s and 1940s, lobsters and crabs were plentiful off the Dalkey coastline and it was usual, as well as commonplace, for fishermen to receive 50s for a lot of thirteen lobsters, with 30s for a second lot.

During the 1940s and 1950s, the most commonly used boats in the harbour were yawls, just over 5m long, and punts, which were a metre shorter. These boats were mostly built in the inland river port of Athlone and they cost £1 a foot to build, a charge that included delivery to Bulloch Harbour. All the boats were clinker built, which meant that the planks in the hull overlapped, then nailed and roofed. The other type of wooden boat is a carvel, where the planks are placed side by side instead of overlapping. But when fishermen at Bulloch Harbour wanted to hire a boat for a day's fishing, the preferred choice was a punt, as it was smaller, more easily manoeuvred and was less tiring to row over long periods of time. The cost of hiring a boat then was 2s an hour, or 2/6d if you wanted someone to do the rowing for you. On the right-hand side of the pier stood what were long known as the 'fishermen's huts', built well over a century ago. The first such hut on the pier was black and was owned by the Dublin Port and Docks company, now known simply as the Dublin Port Company. But this wasn't the first shed in line in the harbour, as a previous shed on the site had been occupied by the Sea Scouts in Dalkey and the Bulloch Rowing Club. Next to the port company shed was one from where the Sandycove Rowing Club operated, while the third shed, built around 1960, housed the Dublin City Sea Anglers' Club.

Bulloch Harbour, since it was built 200 years ago, at around the same time as the harbour in Kingstown, now Dún Laoghaire, has seen many changes. During the nineteenth century, the coal yards were an important feature, where coal was unloaded for local fireplaces. In turn, these coal yards were replaced by some small local boat building yards, but these too have vanished. But the bollards survived the passing of time and in the early twentieth century, the bollards and the shackles were used to secure the coal and stone boats that used the harbour.

But Bulloch Harbour has managed to survive the negative aspects of its location. When there's a strong north-easterly gale, the harbour cannot function. When the weather gets really bad, the sight of the pier being assaulted by high waves, often six or more metres high, is awesome indeed. When strong winds hit the harbour, the private boats often moored in Bulloch Harbour have to be taken out of the water and hauled to safety on the pier itself. The other big disadvantage to Bulloch Harbour is that about 100 metres out to sea from the pier is a rock, clearly seen at spring tides, but very difficult to spot at other times.

These days, Bulloch Harbour has become less known for its maritime activities than for the various development proposals for the harbour itself as well as close to the harbour, that have raised the ire of many local people and led to scores of planning objections.

THE DALKEY ARCHIVE

The Dalkey Archive is a novel by the Irish writer Flann O'Brien, otherwise known as Myles na Gopaleen. It was published in 1964 and was his fifth and final novel, which came out two years before his death. The year after it came out, it was adapted for the stage by Hugh Leonard under the title *The Saints Go Cycling In*.

This book, *The Dalkey Archive*, was published by MacGibbon & Kee in London. It features a mad scientist, De Selby, who tries to destroy the world by extracting all the oxygen from the air. He also creates many strange inventions, one of which is a time-travelling machine which he uses to age his whiskey, so that distillations that would normally take decades to mature did so in a matter of hours. St Augustine and James Joyce both have speaking parts in the novel. James Joyce, who in the novel had forged his own obituary to escape being drafted into the military during the Second World War, is seen working as a bartender in a small pub. St Augustine, on the other hand, appears in a magical underwater cave and has a conversation with De Selby.

Many of the main elements of the book, especially the character of De Selby, the eccentric policeman and the atomic theory of the bicycle, were taken from Flann O'Brien's much earlier novel, *The Third Policeman*, because he hadn't been able to get it published.

Among the targets of O'Brien's derision are religiosity, intellectual abstractions, Einstein's views on time and relativity, and the lives and works of both St Augustine and James Joyce. All the metaphysical chaos of the book is set in Dalkey in the late 1940s.

In the US, a publishing house called the Dalkey Archive Press, in honour of Flann O'Brien's novel, was set up in Chicago in 1984. Its main emphasis has always been on literary fiction, mostly modernist or post-modernist in style. But as with Flann O'Brien's novel, the all-important word is Dalkey, which provides a very specific title for both the novel and for the publishers.

16

THE KING OF DALKEY

It's many years since the subjects of the King of Dalkey have met their monarch, a role that involved considerable festivities at the investitures. It dates back to the late eighteenth century and while it was only revived on rare occasions during the twentieth century, it seems as if it's destined to remain in the history books for ever more.

One of the most recently crowned kings, and that was back in 1975, was John O'Donovan, a music critic and presenter for many years of the RTÉ Radio 1 series, Dear Sir or Madam, based on listeners' letters. When he was crowned King of Dalkey on 12 November 1975, the festivities took place amid a dinner at the old Coliemore Hotel in Dalkey. The menu presented some difficulties, as John O'Donovan was a teetotal vegetarian, so he eschewed all the usual trappings of the Dalkey monarchy and their meat-laden feasts accompanied by vast servings of wine.

Another Dalkey king in more recent times was a Killiney man, Norman Judd, who adopted a boar's head on a white background as his pennant. One of the most famous men to have been crowned King of Dalkey, on the rare occasions the ceremony was enacted during the twentieth century, was Noel Purcell, a well-known Dublin-born actor who became renowned in many movie parts, especially for his very distinctive beard. When he was making his coronation speech in 1945, he urged the publicans of Dalkey to lower the price of a pint by one penny, a suggestion that was surreptitiously ignored.

All the people who took part in these coronations during the twentieth century were dressed in eighteenth-century costumes, hired from a theatrical costumier in Dublin. The proceedings of Coronation Day were often described as a 'bit of gas' and an occasion on which the all-male entourages – no women ever took part– could get well and truly locked with the generosity of all the drink poured during the course of the day and evening.

The full title of the King of Dalkey was most impressive, quite a mouthful even for someone in the vanguard of sobriety. It read as follows:

> King of Dalkey, emperor of the Muglins, Prince of the Holy Island of Magee, Baron of Bulloch, Seigneur of Sandycove, Defender of the Faith and Respecter of All Others, Elector of Lambay and Ireland's Eye, and Sovereign of the Most Illustrious Order of the Lobster and the Periwinkle.

In the late eighteenth century, the Freemen of Dalkey inherited the right to elect the King of Dalkey. They took over this right in 1787 from bored young bloods in Dublin, who had formed a club into which they inveigled poets, thinkers, wits and writers. They had a parliament called the Pimlico Parliament, named after a district in the Liberties, and from an assembly room there, they hurled plentiful abuse at the general state of humbug in the country and especially at all the pompous hacks and journeymen who laboured in the British administration at Dublin Castle. Some of the people they enrolled were well-known, such as Thomas Moore, who wrote satirical verses for them, while John Philpott Curran, the lawyer who defended many United Irishmen, and was the father of Sarah Curran, wrote many screeds on their behalf.

In 1791, the first person the Freemen of Dalkey elected as King of Dalkey was Stephen Armitage, a pawnbroker and printer who also happened to be very anti-establishment. He was elected for no particular reason, except that it was a good occasion to poke fun at the established standards of the time and especially at all the extraordinary fawning over British royalty.

He soon discovered the pitfalls. When his barge was on a starboard tack to Dalkey Island, taking him to the seat of his 'royal' title, it passed a man-of-war belonging to the Royal

Navy. The King of Dalkey ordered that a cannon be fired in salute and in return, the captain of the naval ship dipped his colours and ordered a 21-gun salute. Questions soon came up in the House of Commons in London as to why a captain of the Royal Navy had paid homage on the high seas to the enemies and disrespecters of the proper king, the one who sat on the throne in London. The captain was promptly relieved of his command.

On another occasion, King Stephen published a proclamation in which he said he was legally permitted to import 10,000 hogsheads, duty free. The King of Dalkey was duly summoned before the Lord Chancellor, who asked him what the emoluments of his office were. The King of Dalkey replied: 'I am allowed to import 10,000 hogsheads'. The Chancellor replied, 'Hogsheads of what?' to which the King of Dalkey replied, 'Saltwater'.

Just over a century later came another coronation that went down in history. On 1 June 1901, the Dalkey branch of the Gaelic League organised the coronation of the league's president, Douglas Hyde, who later became the first president of Ireland. The authorities in Dublin Castle reacted in their usual high-handed fashion and issued a Royal Proclamation banning the coronation. However, the proclamation didn't have the slightest effect, as the Gaelic Leaguers in Dalkey went ahead anyway. Hundreds of day-trippers came out to Dalkey from Dublin, facilitated by a special 8*d* excursion fare on the railway. Local boats then ferried them from Coliemore Harbour for 5*d* return. A procession of pipers and Druids was organised on Dalkey Island and at 4 p.m. that afternoon, a public meeting on the island was addressed by several Gaelic League members, including E.A. Fournier, the president of the Dalkey branch.

Sadly, soon after that, the coronation of the King of Dalkey faded into disuse and remarkably few gatherings were held during the rest of the twentieth century and none at all in the first twenty years of the twenty-first century. Whether this ancient custom of frivolity and fun can ever be revived is likely to remain a subject of late-night discussion in Dalkey's various pubs.

FURTHER READING

Ballybrack Local History Group, *The Granite Hills: A Guide to Killiney and Ballybrack* (Co. Dublin, 1982)

Beranger, Gabriel, *Dalkey's Castles* (drawings) (Dublin, 1766)

Edwards, B.L., *Dalkey: A Short Account of the Town* (Dublin, 1933)

Elrington Ball, F., *A History of the County Dublin* (Dublin 1928)

Federation of Mountaineering Clubs of Ireland, *Dalkey Rock Climbs* (Dublin, 1979)

Goodbody, Rob, *The Metals: From Dalkey to Dún Laoghaire* (Co. Dublin, 2010)

Kelly, Michael, *Dalkey, County Dublin* (Dublin, 1952)

Kennedy, Gerald, *Guide to the Historic Town of Dalkey* (Co. Mayo, 1996)

Kenny, Bernie, *A Walk in Dalkey* (poems) (Dublin, 2008)

Kenny, Bernie, *Always Dalkey, Always the Sea* (poems) (Dublin, 2011)

Lynam, Joss, *A Guide to Dalkey Quarry* (Dublin, 1999)

McLoughlin, Peter, *Killiney Walks* (Dublin,1989)

Moroney, Canice, *Killiney* (Co. Dublin, 1954)

Mullen, Frank (compiler), Padraig Yeates (ed.), *Dalkey: An Anthology* (Dublin, 2009)

Pearson, Peter, *Between the Mountains and the Sea* (Dublin, 1998)

Seymour, Pauline (ed.), Dalkey United Golden Jubilee, 1953–2003 (Dublin, 2003)